CW00345564

Soho Theatre in association
with the Royal Shakespeare Company presents

by Georgia Fitch

Fit and Proper People had its world premiere at Soho Theatre,
London, on 7 October 2011

Soho Theatre is supported by Arts Council England, John Ellerman
Foundation, Westminster City Council, Harold Hyam Wingate
Foundation

CAST

Lianne/Fatima	Zahra Ahmadi
Michel Gbagbo/Mouftaou	Mark Anthony Brighton
Billy Williams/Shanika	Kerron Darby
Joey/Tommy	Russell Floyd
Anthony Whitechapel	Steven Hartley
Casey Layton	Katy Stephens
Frank Wong/Craig/Mouftaou's wife	David Yip

COMPANY

Director	Steve Marmion
Designer	Tom Piper
Lighting Designer	Ben Ormerod
Sound Designer	Gregory Clarke
Video Designer	Douglas O'Connell
Choreographer	Spencer Soloman
RSC Dramaturg	Pippa Hill
RSC Producer	Kevin Fitzmaurice
Casting Director	Annie Rowe
Costume Supervisor	Sydney Florence
Assistant Director	Lee Griffiths
Set	Object Construction
Production Manager	Ed Wilson
Graphic Design (Advertising Hoardings)	Andy Williams
Company Stage Manager	Gilda Frost
Deputy Stage Manager	Sarah Jenkins
Assistant Stage Manager	Nicola Morris

BIOGRAPHIES

CAST

ZAHRA AHMADI
Theatre includes:
THIS WIDE NIGHT (Gothenburg English Speaking Theatre); SISTERS (Crucible Sheffield); ISFAHAN CALLING (Old Red Lion); KING OF HEARTS (Out of Joint, Hampstead Theatre); THE DAUGHTER (Wedding Collective); HYSTERIA (Northcott Theatre Exeter); COOKING WITH ELVIS (Edinburgh Fringe); WHERE ARE YOU GONE JIMMY TREVENNA? (Edinburgh Fringe) and as Assistant Director GLADIATOR GAMES (Sheffield Theatres/Theatre Royal Stratford East).
Television includes:
THE INCREASINGLY POOR DECISIONS OF TODD MARGARET; BELLAMY'S PEOPLE; DOCTORS; EASTENDERS; BRITZ; TRIAL & RETRIBUTION X.
Film includes:
TAMARA DREWE; AFTER THESE MESSAGES; RUSHMART; THE PECULIAR CASE OF DR ALEXA.

MARK ANTHONY BRIGHTON
Theatre includes:
THE TIN HORIZON (Theatre 503); JUNIOR'S STORY (The Oval House Theatre); WHAT THE BUTLER SAW, ONCE IN A LIFETIME, STRANGEST KIND OF ROMANCE, AS YOU LIKE IT, KING LEAR, THE SEAGULL, THE LADY OF LARKSPUR LOTION, ENTERTAINING MR SLOANE, THE MASTER BUILDER (Poor School Workhouse Theatre).
Television includes:
MISSING (BBC); HOW NOT TO LIVE YOUR LIFE (BBC3); BANGED UP ABROAD (Raw TV); HOLBY CITY (BBC); SILENT WITNESS (BBC); DOCTORS (BBC); GOLDEN HOUR (Talkback/Thames); CASUALTY (BBC); THE GOSPEL ACCORDING TO JOHN (TGJ Ltd); FINAL DEMAND (BBC); STRANGE (BBC); INSPECTOR LYNLEY MYSTERIES (BBC); IN DEEP (BBC); MY HERO (BBC); THE BILL (Thames); THE HIDDEN CITY (Obahc/Rough Films).
Film includes:
READY WHEN YOU ARE MR MCGILL (Working Title); STAINED GLASS (Moonstone Laboratories); GREEN STREET (Odd Lot Entertainment); DIRTY BRITISH BOYS (Firestorm Pictures).

KERRON DARBY
Theatre includes:
THE KNOWLEDGE, LITTLE PLATOONS (Bush Theatre); BIG RED (Royal Court Theatre – rehearsed reading).
Television includes:
THE BILL, (BBC); CASUALTY (BBC); BEAUTIFUL PEOPLE (BBC); POSTCODE (BBC); SILENT WITNESS (BBC).

RUSSELL FLOYD

Theatre includes:
MAGGIE'S END (Northern Theatre); NEGATIVE SPACE (TheFizzProductions); THE BULLET (Two Bins Productions); DRACULA/OFFICE PARTY (Hull Truck); ACCIDENTAL DEATH OF AN ANARCHIST (Magnificent Theatre Company); A MIDSUMMER NIGHT'S DREAM (MTC); PRIVATES ON PARADE (Westcliff Palace Theatre); SIR COURTLY NICE (Royal Shakespeare Company); GOING TO A PARTY (National Theatre); TWELFTH NIGHT (Orchard Theatre Company); UP AND UNDER (Swansea Theatre Royal); PLEASE ONE PLEASE ALL (Bristol Express); THE PROMISE, THE IMPORTANCE OF BEING EARNEST, THE GLASS MENAGERIE (Oxford); MACBETH, ROMEO AND JULIET, WAIT UNTIL DARK (Ipswich Wolsey Theatre); THEFT (National Theatre Studio); HAMLET (Sherman Theatre Cardiff).
Television includes:
CASUALTY (BBC); DOCTORS (BBC); DREAM TEAM (Hewland International); THE BILL (Thames Television/Pearson Television); EASTENDERS (BBC); FRANK STUBBS PRESENTS (LWT); LONDON'S BURNING (LWT); THE FRIDGE (HTV); MARTIN AMIS FILM (CBC); DEFROSTING THE FRIDGE (BBC 2).
Radio includes:
EXAMINATION DAY (BBC); BODY LANGUAGE (BBC); ESCAPE FROM NORMAN'S CROSS (BBC); MASTER AND COMMANDER (BBC); MUTINY ON THE BOUNTY (BBC); OVER THE WALL (BBC); BOMBER (BBC); IMMIGRANTS (BBC); TRIAL OF CHARLES 1 (BBC); SIR COURTLY NICE (BBC); AUDIENCE (BBC).
Film includes:
END GAME (Various Films); ASCENDANCY (Channel 4 Television).

STEVEN HARTLEY

Theatre includes:
OLIVER (Theatre Royal Drury Lane); DIRTY DANCING (Aldwych Theatre); INSIGNIFICANCE (Theatre Royal Northampton/Brighton Festival); OLIVER (London Palladium/North American tour); AN EVENING WITH GARY LINEKER (Vaudaville/Number 1 Tour); MILLFIRE (Bush Theatre/Riverside Studios); SMOKE (Manchester Royal Exchange); REBECCA (Colchester Mercury/Number 1 Tour); BABES IN ARMS (Plymouth Theatre Royal/Number 1 Tour); NORMAL HEART, TOM JONES, SEXUAL PERVERSITY IN CHICAGO, PIAF, FUNNY PECULIAR, ANNIE, TRAFFORD TANZI, HAYFEVER (Colchester Mercury).
Television includes:
VERA; MERLIN; THE CUT; MARPLE; CASUALTY; STRICTLY CONFIDENTIAL; DOCTORS; HOLBY CITY; WHERE THE HEART IS; THE BILL; TRIAL AND RETRIBUTION; SHARMAN; THE GOVERNOR; PIE IN THE SKY; BAD BOYS; YOUNG INDIANNA JONES; RUMBLE; MARRIED WITH CHILDREN; PRESS GANG; ZORRO; EASTENDERS; OUT OF ORDER; CAFÉ SOCIETY.
Steven has been nominated

for Best Actor at the National Television Awards and the British Soap Awards.
Film includes:
DESERTER; THE WALKER; COLUMBUS THE DISCOVERY; SPLIT SECOND; DOG OF FLANDERS; CHERNOBYL: THE FINAL WARNING; YOUNG TOSCANINNI; QUEENS OF CLUBS.

KATY STEPHENS
Theatre includes:
AS YOU LIKE IT, THE GRAIN STORE, KING LEAR, ANTONY AND CLEOPATRA, HENRY VI PARTS 1, 2 AND 3, RICHARD II, RICHARD III, HENRY IV PART 2, HENRY V (Royal Shakespeare Company); TAMBURLAINE (Bristol Old Vic/Barbican); SILENCE (RSC/Filter/Hampstead); MINE (Shared Experience); THE SEAGULL, ION, MACBETH, THE WHITE DEVIL, OH! WHAT A LOVELY WAR, THE THREE SISTERS, THE EUROPEANS, CAUCASIAN CHALK CIRCLE, BLOOD WEDDING, THE RECRUITING OFFICER (Mercury, Colchester); TWELFTH NIGHT, SLEEPING BEAUTY, OUR DAY OUT, SILAS MARNER (Belgrade, Coventry); DAVID COPPERFIELD, I DON'T WANT TO SET THE WORLD ON FIRE (New Victoria, Newcastle-under-Lyme), A MIDSUMMER NIGHT'S DREAM (Orchard Theatre Company).
Television includes:
THE BILL (ITV); LONDON'S BURNING (LWT); FUN SONG FACTORY (CITV); ELLINGTON (ITV).
Film includes:
RELATIVE VALUES (Overseas Film Group).

DAVID YIP
Theatre includes:
GOLD MOUNTAIN (Unity Theatre, Les Deux Mondes Montreal); CHUN LI THE LEGEND OF KUNG FU (London Coliseum); THE KING AND I (Royal Albert Hall); TURANDOT (Hampstead Theatre); KING LEAR (Yellow Earth/RSC UK/Shanghai); HAMLET (Singapore Rep Company); ALADDIN (Theatre Royal, Brighton); THE LIFE OF THE WORLD TO COME (Almeida Theatre); WHITE WOMAN (Bush/Abbey Theatre); FRAUDS (Dublin Abbey Theatre); DON'T GO AWAY MAD (Donmar Warehouse); JULIUS CAESAR (Bristol Old Vic); MADE IN BANGKOK (Aldwych); THE KNACK (National Tour); BURIED TREASURE (Tricycle Theatre);
Film includes: ACT OF GRACE; TRIAGE; MY KINGDOM; ENTRAPMENT; HAMLET; HAWKS; EMPIRE OF THE SUN; PING PONG; JAMES BOND: A VIEW TO A KILL; INDIANA JONES AND THE TEMPLE OF DOOM.
Television Includes:
SPIRIT WARRIORS; THE LIVERPOOL NATIVITY; CASUALTY; INTERGALACTIC PATRICK; THE BILL; MERSEYBEAT II; OSCAR CHARLIE; SNAKE BOY AND SANDCASTLES; THE CHINESE DETECTIVE.

see www.davidyip.co.uk for more details.

GEORGIA FITCH – WRITER

Georgia Fitch's plays for the stage include ADRENALIN... HEART (Bush Theatre, London 2002, 2004 and Tokyo International Theatre Festival); I LIKE MINE WITH A KISS (Bush Theatre, London 2007); DIRTY DIRTY PRINCESS (National Theatre/Connections 2009) FIT AND PROPER PEOPLE was shortlisted for the Susan Smith Blackburn Award earlier this year.

Earlier theatre work with Angels Theatre Company includes THE FOOTBALLER'S WIFE* (Riverside Studios/ Royal Festival Hall 1997); COME DANCING*, ARRIVALS (Old Red Lion, London 1999).

For Radio (BBC) plays include: ROMEO AND JULIET IN SOUTHWARK, THE MOTHER OF..., UNTITLED LOVER, I MET A BOY, FORTUNE'S ALWAYS HIDING and ADRENALIN... HEART.

Other work includes DIS-ASSEMBLY (Serpentine Gallery 2006, with Runa Islam).

*Co – written with Tracy O'Flaherty.

STEVE MARMION – DIRECTOR

Steve is the Artistic Director of Soho Theatre.

Theatre includes: REALISM, MONGREL ISLAND (Soho Theatre); MACBETH (Open Air Theatre, Regent's Park); EDWARD GANT'S AMAZING FEATS OF LONELINESS (Headlong/Soho Theatre); VINCENT RIVER (Brits off Broadway, New York); FAUSTUS (Headlong); METROPOLIS (Bath Theatre Royal); ALADDIN, JACK AND THE BEANSTALK, DICK WHITTINGTON (Lyric Hammersmith); ONLY THE BRAVE, THE ENTIRE HISTORY OF CABARET, LATE NIGHT GIMP FIGHT (Edinburgh Festival Fringe); LOCK UP (National Theatre Education); TEMPEST 2000 (Sherman); A DATE TO REMEMBER (Soho Theatre Studio); MAD MARGARET'S REVENGE (London One Act Festival/ Edinburgh Festival Fringe); MADAM BUTTERFLY'S CHILD (Pleasance/ Greenwich Festival/ Hong Kong Festival/ London One Act Festival – Winner of Best Overall Production/ Edinburgh Festival Fringe); CALIBAN'S ISLAND (Tour/ Edinburgh Festival Fringe); 97 – HILLSBOROUGH (Tour/ Edinburgh Festival Fringe); GHETTO (Watford Palace Theatre); LITTLE NELL, IMAGES OF A LONELY POET'S WAR (E15); LUNCHTIME LOTTERY (Plush Productions); SLEEPING BEAUTY, MIRANDA'S MAGIC MIRROR, TINY TALES (Stephen

Joseph Theatre, Scarborough); TEAM SPIRIT, SK8 – A HIP HOP MUSICAL, MULTIPLEX (Theatre Royal Plymouth).

TOM PIPER – DESIGNER

Tom is Associate Designer at the RSC. He has won the London Fringe Best Design Award twice and an Olivier Award for his costume designs for THE HISTORIES.
For the RSC: THE BROKEN HEART, SPRING AWAKENING, A PATRIOT FOR ME, MUCH ADO ABOUT NOTHING, THE SPANISH TRAGEDY, BARTHOLOMEW FAIR, MEASURE FOR MEASURE, TROILUS AND CRESSIDA, A MONTH IN THE COUNTRY, A MIDSUMMER NIGHT'S DREAM, ROMEO AND JULIET, HENRY VI, RICHARD III, THE TEMPEST, KING LEAR, TWELFTH NIGHT, HAMLET, THE HISTORIES, AS YOU LIKE IT, THE DRUNKS, THE GRAIN STORE, ANTONY AND CLEOPATRA, MACBETH and CITY MADAM.
Other theatre includes: THE BIRTHDAY PARTY, BLINDED BY THE SUN, OH! WHAT A LOVELY WAR (RNT); MISS JULIE (Theatre Royal Haymarket); FRAME 312, A LIE OF THE MIND, THREE DAYS OF RAIN, HELPLESS (Donmar); PANTS, MINCE, TWELFTH NIGHT, DUCHESS OF MALFI, HAPPY DAYS (Dundee Rep); LES LIAISONS DANGEREUSES, LOOT (Bristol Old Vic); STIFF!, THE MASTER BUILDER (Lyceum, Edinburgh); THE DANNY CROWE SHOW (Bush); THE SPIRIT OF ANNIE ROSS (Gate Theatre, Dublin); THE FROGS, THE CHERRY ORCHARD (Nottingham Playhouse); DEALER'S CHOICE (Theater in der Josefstadt, Vienna); SCISSOR HAPPY (Duchess Theatre); WALLACE AND GROMIT – A GRAND NIGHT OUT (Peacock Theatre and tour); KINDERTRANSPORT (Vaudeville, Watford and Soho Theatre); THE CRUCIBLE, SIX CHARACTERS IN SEARCH OF AN AUTHOR, THE LAST DAYS OF A RELUCTANT TYRANT, THE PLOUGH AND THE STARS (Abbey Theatre, Dublin); BACKPAY, COCKROACH WHO?, (Royal Court); WAKING, TULIPFUTURES, RIPPED, MY GOAT, ROCKSTATION, OPENING 4 PLAY SEASON (Soho Theatre); ENDGAME, DUMBSTRUCK, MACBETH (Tron Theatre, Glasgow); THE PRICE (Theatre Royal York); THE WAY OF THE WORLD, SPYSKI (Lyric Hammersmith); THE DUCHESS OF MALFI (Wyndham's, Greenwich and tour); SWEET PANIC, THE PHILANDERER, DISPOSING OF THE BODY (Hampstead Theatre); INSIGNIFICANCE (Sheffield Theatres); BABETTE'S FEAST (Royal Opera House); AS YOU LIKE IT, THE TEMPEST, RICHARD III (Bridge project BAM and Old Vic); ZORRO THE MUSICAL (Garrick, Paris, Tokyo, Moscow, Holland); MACBETH, FALSTAFF (Scottish Opera).

BEN ORMEROD – LIGHTING DESIGNER

Theatre includes: LOYALTY (Hampstead); ONASSIS (West End); ZORRO! (West End/International); THE PHOENIX OF MADRID & IPHIGENIA (Bath Theatre Royal); SERIOUS MONEY, LAST EASTER (Birmingham); DIMETOS (Donmar); TWO MEN OF FLORENCE (Boston); SANCTUARY LAMP (B*spoke); MACBETH (West End); THE CRUCIBLE (Lyric Belfast); TRANSLATIONS, THE LAST DAYS OF A RELUCTANT TYRANT (Abbey, Dublin); THE CHANGELING, HEDDA GABLER, THE DOLL'S HOUSE, JOHN GABRIEL BORKMANN (ETT); CARMEN (Pimlico); THE LEENANE TRILOGY (Druid); MACBETH, HENRY V, JULIUS CAESAR, THE SPANISH GOLDEN AGE SEASON (RSC); BENT, UNCLE VANYA, THE WINTER'S TALE, IN REMEMBRANCE OF THINGS PAST (National); RICHARD III, COMEDY OF ERRORS (Propeller); ROSE RAGE (New York/Chicago).

Forthcoming theatre includes: THE HERESY OF LOVE (RSC); HENRY V, THE WINTER'S TALE (Propeller).

Opera and dance includes: Productions for Scottish Opera, ENO, Opera North, Cedar Lake New York and, most recently, LA TRAVIATA (Danish National Opera).

Ben designed the lighting for the Calico Museum of Textiles, Ahmedabad, directed Athol Fugard's DIMETOS (Gate, London) and adapted four films from Kieslowski's DEKALOG for E15.

GREGORY CLARKE – SOUND DESIGNER

Gregory won a Tony Award for Best Sound Design in a Play for EQUUS and received the New York Drama Desk Award for Outstanding Sound Design for JOURNEY'S END.

Theatre includes: TWELFTH NIGHT, EARTHQUAKES IN LONDON (National Theatre); A MIDSUMMER NIGHT'S DREAM, THE MERCHANT OF VENICE, CYMBELINE, GREAT EXPECTATIONS, CORIOLANUS, MERRY WIVES OF WINDSOR, TANTALUS (Royal Shakespeare Company); A FLEA IN HER EAR, SIX DEGREES OF SEPARATION, NATIONAL ANTHEMS (Old Vic); PENELOPE (Druid Theatre); TESTAMENT, MISTERMAN (Landmark Productions); HUNDREDS & THOUSANDS (Soho Theatre); BEDROOM FARCE, RAIN MAN (West End); GOODNIGHT MISTER TOM, A MONTH IN THE COUNTRY, CAUGHT MY DEATH IN VENICE, NATHAN THE WISE, SONG OF SINGAPORE (Chichester); PETER PAN (Kensington Gardens/O2 Centre/US Tour); A MIDSUMMER NIGHT'S DREAM, TREASURE ISLAND, BEDROOM FARCE/MISS JULIE, THE BROWNING VERSION, LOVE'S LABOUR'S LOST (Rose); THE PHILANTHROPIST (American Airlines, Broadway);

MY DAD'S A BIRDMAN, BAY (Young Vic); FOR KING AND COUNTRY (UK Tour); THE ELECTRIC BALLROOM (Riverside Studios); LOOT (Tricycle Theatre); CROWN MATRIMONIAL, RING AROUND THE MOON (Act Productions); EQUUS (Gielgud & Broadway); HENRY IV (Parts I and II); THIS HAPPY BREED, JEFFREY BERNARD IS UNWELL, BLITHE SPIRIT, THE RIVALS, HEDDA GABLER, THE WINSLOW BOY, BALMORAL, THE BROWNING VERSION, SWANSONG, THE APPLE CART, HOME, HOW THE OTHER HALF LOVES, VICTORY, OLD TIMES, AMY'S VIEW, YOU NEVER CAN TELL, HMS PINAFORE, MUCH ADO ABOUT NOTHING, THE DRESSER, AS YOU LIKE IT (Theatre Royal Bath); WHERE THERE'S A WILL, UNCLE VANYA (ETT); LITTLE WOLF, IN THE CLUB, THE GLASS ROOM, EVERYTHING IS ILLUMINATED, CLEVER DICK, WHEN THE NIGHT BEGINS, REVELATIONS, THE MATHS TUTOR (Hampstead); PETER PAN, KRINDLEKRAX (Birmingham Rep); CLOUD 9 (Almeida); THE BOYFRIEND, LADY BE GOOD, A MIDSUMMER NIGHT'S DREAM, MACBETH, TWELFTH NIGHT, CYMBELINE (NSC); A VOYAGE ROUND MY FATHER (Donmar); HAY FEVER (Haymarket); NIGHTS AT THE CIRCUS (Lyric Hammersmith).

DOUGLAS O'CONNELL – VIDEO DESIGNER
Douglas began his career working in Off Broadway and regional theatre throughout New York. In Chicago, as a member of Redmoon Theatre, he received awards in design for his work at the renowned Steppenwolf Studio Theater. Theatre includes: SILENCE (Royal Shakespeare Company/Filter); DANCE MARATHON (Barbican and Traverse Theatre/Edinburgh Festival Fringe Festival); I HAVE A DREAM (Polka Theatre); TURN OF THE SCREW, MONSTERS (Arcola Theatre); NO WISE MEN (Peepolykus/ Liverpool Playhouse); BALLET SHOES (Peacock Theatre); BEHUD, THIS ISN'T ROMANCE (Soho Theatre); THIEF OF BAGDAD (Royal Ballet London); 4:48 PSYCHOSIS (Cumbernauld Theatre, Glasgow); FIGHT FACE, SARAJEVO STORY (Lyric Theatre); SATURDAY NIGHT SUNDAY MORNING (Harrogate Theatre/ Oldham Theatre); BACK AT YOU (BAC); HERE'S WHAT MY BODY DID ONE DAY (Pleasance Theatre/ Tour); PASSIONATE ALLIANCE (Cardboard Citizens/Emergency Exit Arts); INVERTIGO (Visions Festival, Brighton).

SPENCER SOLOMAN – CHOREOGRAPHER

As resident/associate choreographer – theatre includes:
HAIRSPRAY (Shaftesbury Theatre); GUYS AND DOLLS (Piccadilly Theatre); ON YOUR TOES (Royal Festival Hall); A FUNNY THING HAPPENED ON THE WAY TO THE FORUM (National Theatre).
As assistant choreographer – theatre includes:
HOW TO SUCCEED IN BUSINESS WITHOUT REALLY TRYING (Al Hirstfeld Theatre, Broadway); PARADE (Donmar Warehouse); CANDIDE (La Scala, Milan); PARDON MY ENGLISH (New York).
As assistant choreographer - television includes:
GREASE IS THE WORD (ITV).

THANK YOU

Soho Theatre and Royal Shakespeare Company would like to acknowledge the generous support of the following:
Eddie Chan, Chinese National Healthy Living Centre
Lyric Hammersmith
MAC
Daisy Chiara Marcuzzi
Graham Morris
Newman Displays
Object Construction
Stage Sound Services
Steeldeck Ltd
Wrights Pies Ltd
Heather Rabbatts
all at Millwall FC

Bang in the creative heart of London, Soho Theatre is a major new writing theatre and a writers' development organisation of national significance. With a programme spanning theatre, comedy, cabaret and writers' events and home to a lively bar, Soho Theatre is one of the most vibrant venues on London's cultural scene.

Soho Theatre owns its own Central London venue housing the intimate 150-seat Soho Theatre, our 90-seat Soho Upstairs and our new 1950s New York meets Berliner cabaret space, Soho Downstairs. Under the joint leadership of Soho's Artistic Director Steve Marmion and Executive Director Mark Godfrey, Soho Theatre now welcomes over 100,000 people a year.

'If Marmion's zippy opening production in the main house is anything to go by, there's going to be some punchy new writing to savour.' Evening Standard

'Soho Theatre's new basement cabaret space, which has the feel of a comedy club (tables, its own bar) - expect it to become an important room for comedy in the capital' Times

THE TERRACE BAR
Drinks can be taken into the auditorium and are available from the Terrace Bar on the second floor.

SOHO THEATRE ONLINE
Giving you the latest information and previews of upcoming shows, Soho Theatre can be found on facebook, twitter and youtube as well as at sohotheatre.com

EMAIL INFORMATION LIST
For regular programme updates and offers visit sohotheatre.com/mailing

HIRING THE THEATRE
An ideal venue for a variety of events, we have a range of spaces available for hire in the heart of the West End. Meetings, conferences, parties, civil ceremonies, rehearsed readings and showcases with support from our professional theatre team to assist in your events' success.

For more information, please see our website sohotheatre.com/hires or to hire space at Soho Theatre, email hires@sohotheatre.com and to book an event in Soho Theatre Bar, email sohotheatrebar@sohotheatre.com or ring 0207 434 9393.

Soho Theatre is supported by: ACE, John Ellerman Foundation, Westminster City Council, Harold Hyam Wingate Foundation

Registered Charity No: 267234

THANK YOU

We gratefully acknowledge the following supporters who are an intrinsic part of Soho Theatre – thank you.

Our supporters share with us a common goal and help us to achieve our mission: to source new work, to discover and nurture new talent and to produce profound and exciting theatre, comedy and cabaret.

Without your support, we would not be able to continue to achieve the diversity of our current programme, innovative community work and pioneering work through our Writer's Centre.

To find out how you can be involved in Soho Theatre, please contact the Development Team on 020 7478 0111, development@sohotheatre.com or visit www.sohotheatre.com.

Sponsors
Granta

Principal Supporters
Nicholas Allott
Daniel and Joanna Friel
Mr & Mrs Jack and Linda Keenan
Amelia and Neil Mendoza
Lady Sainsbury of Turville
Mrs Carolyn Ward

Corporate Supporters
Cameron Mackintosh Ltd

In-Kind Sponsors
Latham & Watkins
Goodman Derrick LLP
The Groucho Club
SSE Audio
Soundcraft
Nexo
Wrights Pies Ltd

Trusts & Foundations
Andor Charitable Trust
BBC Children in Need
Boris Karloff Charitable Foundation
City Bridge Trust
David and Elaine Potter Foundation
Earmark Trust
8th Earl of Sandwich Memorial Trust
Fenton Arts Trust
Harold Hyam Wingate Foundation
John Ellerman Foundation
JP Getty Junior Charitable Trust
Equity Charitable Trust
Eranda Foundation
Mackintosh Foundation
Rose Foundation

Foundation for Sport and the Arts
Sir Siegmund Warburg's Voluntary Settlement
Teale Charitable Trust
The Thistle Trust
Miss Hazel M Wood Charitable Trust

Soho Theatre Best Friends
David Day
Hedley and Fiona Goldberg
Hils Jago, Amused Moose Comedy
Andrew and Jane McManus
Ann Stanton

Soho Theatre Dear Friends
Natalie Bakova
Quentin Bargate
Isobel and Michael Holland

Soho Good Friends
Neil and Sarah Brener
David Brooks
Gayle Bryans
Mathew Burkitt
Chris Carter
Victoria Carr
Jeremy Conway
Sharon Eva Degen
Geoffrey Eagland
Gail and Michael Flesch
Alban Gordon
Doug Hawkins
James Hogan and Charles Glanville
Laurence Humphreys-Davies
Etan Ilfeld
Jennifer Jacobs
Amanda Mason
Mr & Mrs Roger Myddelton
Linda O'Callaghan
Alan Pardoe
Tom Schoon and Philippa Moore
Barry Serjent
Nigel Silby
Lesley Symons
Dr Sean White
Liz Young
Plus those supporters who wish to stay anonymous.

Our other Friends:
Thank you also to the many Soho Friends we are unable to list here.

For a full list of our supporters, please visit sohotheatre.com

This list is correct as of Wednesday 21 September 2011

Registered Charity: 267234

 Supported by
ARTS COUNCIL ENGLAND

NEW WORK AT THE RSC

Georgia Fitch's play *Fit And Proper People* was commissioned by the Royal Shakespeare Company and developed by the RSC Studio.

We invite writers to spend time with us in our rehearsal rooms, with our actors and practitioners. Alongside developing their own plays, we invite them to contribute dramaturgically to both our main stage Shakespeare productions and our Young People's Shakespeare. We invite writers to develop more experimental projects in the RSC Studio.

We believe that our writers help to establish a creative culture within the Company which both inspires new work and creates an ever more urgent sense of enquiry into the classics. The benefits work both ways. With our writers, our actors naturally learn the language of dramaturgical intervention and sharpen their interpretation of roles. Our writers benefit from re-discovering the stagecraft and theatre skills that have been lost over time. They regain the knack of writing roles for leading actors. They become hungry to use classical structures to power up their plays.

The RSC Literary Department is generously supported by THE DRUE HEINZ TRUST

ABOUT THE ROYAL SHAKESPEARE COMPANY

The Royal Shakespeare Company at Stratford-upon-Avon was formed in 1960 and gained its Royal Charter in 1961. This year we celebrate 50 years as a home for Shakespeare's work, the wider classical repertoire and new plays.

Patron
Her Majesty the Queen

President
His Royal Highness The Prince of Wales

Deputy President
Sir Geoffrey Cass

Artistic Director
Michael Boyd

Executive Director
Vikki Heywood

Board
Sir Christopher Bland (Chairman)
Professor Jonathan Bate CBE FBA FRSL
Michael Boyd (Artistic Director)
Damon Buffini
David Burbidge OBE
Jane Drabble OBE
Noma Dumezweni
Mark Foster
Gilla Harris
Vikki Heywood (Executive Director)
John Hornby
Baroness McIntosh of Hudnall
Paul Morrell OBE
Tim Pigott-Smith
Neil Rami
Lady Sainsbury of Turville (Deputy Chairman)

The RSC is grateful for the significant support of its principle funder, Arts Council England, without which our work would not be possible. Around 50 per cent of the RSC's income is self-generated from Box Office sales, sponsorship, donations, enterprise and partnerships with other organisations.

Supported by
ARTS COUNCIL ENGLAND

Georgia Fitch

FIT AND PROPER PEOPLE

OBERON BOOKS
LONDON

WWW.OBERONBOOKS.COM

First published in 2011 by Oberon Books Ltd
521 Caledonian Road, London N7 9RH
Tel: +44 (0) 20 7607 3637 / Fax: +44 (0) 20 7607 3629
e-mail: info@oberonbooks.com
www.oberonbooks.com

A catalogue record for this book is available from the British
Library.

ISBN: 978-1-84943-229-0

Cover design by Michael Windsor-Ungureanu

Printed and bound by CPI Group (UK) Ltd, Croydon, CR0 4YY.

Author's note

'Some people say football is a matter of life and death. I don't like that attitude, it's more important than that.'

Bill Shankley

This is a work of fiction, and although inspired by real events, changes have been made for dramatic effect.

Thanks to:

Steve Marmion, Charlie Briggs, Mark Godfrey, Nina Steiger and all at Soho. Michael Boyd, Jeanie O'Hare, Pippa Hill, Clare Lizzimore, Kevin Fitzmaurice, Tom Piper, and all at RSC. My lovely cast, and all the great actors who took part in the workshops, especially David Kennedy. Annie Rowe, the gifted creatives and the crew. The Susan Smith Blackburn Prize, Dee England, and the many people who gave up their time, to tell me their stories.

For a more journalistic reading on this subject, I would highly suggest Tom Bower's *Broken Dreams* and David Conn's *The Beautiful Game?*.

For my dad, George Fitch.

Characters

CASEY LAYTON
London/white, early forties

FRANK WONG
Chinese, fifties
(Mouftaou's wife, forties/Craig, forties)

ANTHONY WHITECHAPEL
London/white, mid forties

MICHEL GBAGBO
West African, mid to late thirties
(Mouftaou, West African, early sixties)

BILLY WILLIAMS
London/mixed race, late teens
(Razak, West African, mid teens/
Shanika, London, mid teens)

JOEY
London, early forties
(Tommy, Northern, early fifties)

LIANNE
London, late teens
(Fatima, Asian, twenties)

WOMAN IN WHEELCHAIR
fifties

Setting
A football pitch with some screens. A game.

Time
2011

/
indicates an interrupted line

…
indicates that the word/line should be protracted

( )
indicates words which are not spoken

All the major players are on the pitch. CASEY stands on the centre circle and is confident. FATIMA is substituted and on the bench.

(To us.)

CASEY: There are ten steps to living a more balanced life/

FRANK: And being on mission!

CASEY: I have my top five, printed on a card, kept in my pocket...

FRANK: Always!

CASEY: Being grateful, now that's very/

FRANK: Important.

CASEY: Transforming your baggage/

TONY: *(Aside.)* Do we really have to listen to this/

CASEY: Smiling when you can...

TONY: Alright mate?

CASEY: Planning a clear route forward and/

MICHEL: Completing things *(Beat.)*

CASEY: So when I stepped back into my childhood football club, to/

TONY: Set the cat amongst the pigeons/

CASEY: I knew I was on course, I was well on mission and indeed on the road to leaving/

FRANK: My Legacy!

CASEY: So, there was lots and lots of footballing smoke and mirrors and mess, in a club...

JOEY: East London!

BILLY: Innit!

FRANK: Somewhere in the UK.

CASEY: Secure new ownership…

FRANK: Just call me Frankie!

CASEY: *(Acknowledging TONY.)* Metaphorically hoover it all up/

TONY: *(Aside.)* Cloughie loved a bung!

CASEY: Get out Anthony Whitechapel, the manager at/

TONY: *(Aside.)* she's a fucking bitch…

CASEY: Try to save and reinvent a financially sinking ship and get our team and top striker!

BILLY: BILLY WILLIAMS BWAI!

JOEY: Scoring some fucking goals …

CASEY: Our beautiful…increasingly dirty dirty game…of which as an agent/

TONY: She had made a shed load from…

CASEY: Needed the new me now, the entire industry/

JOEY: Made to look like a right bunch of…

CASEY: *(Acknowledging JOEY.)* The fans…

MICHEL: Who bought their satellite packages and kept Mr Murdoch afloat for those first six years…

JOEY: We didn't have much choice…

MICHEL: Always a choice…

CASEY: Were all desperate for a Casey/

FRANK: Layton!

CASEY: I was/

MICHEL: Someone on her side, someone both outside of this somewhat personal project/

CASEY: *(Staring at MICHEL.)* Yet easily…

FRANK: The club, less than an hour before the function where/

CASEY: My new plan was to be launched, as I sat in the/

TONY: Ok, so the room needed a lick of paint!

CASEY: Looking at the photos of the millionaire players in their *Ikea* frames…staring at the peeling magnolia walls…

FRANK: Casey!

CASEY: I decided on not having another frozen chicken drumstick, and my thoughts again turned to/

MICHEL: Michel Gbagbo!

CASEY: I hadn't seen Michel for ages, for him being injured and without a club/

MICHEL: Without an agent/

CASEY: I could lure him in. I knew he had the potential to do what Teddy Sheringham had done for the Hammers, in his more mature years.

TONY: Bring him on for twenty minutes at the end!

MICHEL: 'Come and join me in London', followed by: 'back in the Premiership next season darling?'

CASEY: In football you are/

TONY: Only/

FRANK: Your game/

CASEY: That's the way *it* plays.

MICHEL: Michel texted back/

CASEY: Asking if I was still all about control. We had a few tense exchanges and he finished by sort of/

MICHEL: If you give a handshake to the leopard, next time he will come for an embrace. *(Beat.)* Why now Casey, really why now…

CASEY: I wanted my life to be very different; I wanted things to be out in the open, I craved…

TONY: Power!

MICHEL: My ex was scared.

TONY:

CASEY: I needed to save us from eventual receivership, that we could all finally go global. Frank Wong was now on board/

FRANK: Big big money was in!

CASEY: There was serious business to be done, final bloody/

TONY: Battles still to be won/

CASEY: And the money, the man helping me/

FRANK: If somebody asks me a question, I answer; if they don't ask me a question, I don't answer…

CASEY: Via a world renowned personal and business development guru, via Houston, via a billionaires' breakfast in New York.

MICHEL: Having some fun with his money?

FRANK: Show me clean money…anywhere in the world… show me fucking clean money!

TONY: Frank was well up for embracing the white proletariat consciousness/ speaking like/

JOEY: Me!

CASEY: It was September/

TONY: The transfer window had just closed/

FRANK: And they had already lost half of their opening games.

TONY: We were not promotion favourites, and as long as we could finish above West Ham, that's all the fans wanted!

CASEY: I had never felt more confident – never felt more ready…

(The scene, an imminent press conference, much activity and nerves.)

FRANK: My takeover…it's supposed to be about my takeover!

CASEY: Linda's illness, Tony's antics…have been kept out of the tabloids for this long…

FRANK: This all doesn't feel right…

CASEY: There's no sushi or a small orchestra Frank, because you wanted an authentic experience!

FRANK: Don't take the piss!

CASEY:

FRANK: I am stuck in a grubby hall, now being overshadowed in the press…

CASEY: You are being slightly paranoid/

FRANK: By a silly daft bird/the manager's wife…

CASEY: Linda Whitechapel/

FRANK: In Essex on a fucking drip!

(She moves in closer, studying him.)

CASEY: You said you didn't want too much publicity, which obviously leads to, a lot of digging around.

FRANK: There is a room full of players, fans, press and media…

CASEY: Fantastic…

FRANK: But no manager…

CASEY: We are going to employ a new one aren't we?

FRANK:

CASEY: That's what we agreed.

FRANK: Well…yes and…

CASEY: Yep he keeps us stuck and we are going global!

FRANK: Yeah...

CASEY: Why are you so anxious?

FRANK: I AM NOT!

CASEY: Anthony not turning up only strengthens our case to sack him...

FRANK: Don't say too much alright?

(FRANK exits.)

CASEY: Frank!

(A naked LIANNE steps forward.)

CASEY: How did you get in?

LIANNE: I'm doing the catering...

CASEY: Put your clothes on...

LIANNE: Who the fuck are you?

CASEY: Part of the new regime...management!

LIANNE: What?

CASEY: First and foremost/

LIANNE: What?

CASEY: The club's primary agent...

LIANNE: It's all been arranged and I need to get paid!

CASEY: Don't worry you will be/

LIANNE: Look the players booked me and I need to get fucking paid alright!

(CASEY speaks again to us, LIANNE walks away.)

CASEY: Like Hilary Clinton/

MICHEL: Four hours sleep for many weeks/

CASEY: Not allowing any emotion/

JOEY: I belong here!

MICHEL: To get the better of/

CASEY: Me!

MICHEL: The room was mostly/

CASEY: Nicely filling up/

FRANK: She was getting ready to make the speech that would consolidate everything, highlight/

CASEY: The way forward!

(She looks around the room.)

TONY: People bitching that she was aping Brady/

CASEY: I wouldn't sell my husband twice, just like Karen did, then again I had never/

MICHEL: *(Direct to CASEY.)* Actually married a professional footballer...married anyone?

(Beat.)

CASEY: You see professionally I wanted to focus more on/

FRANK: Pimping for clubs, instead of pimping for boys.

(The scene. BILLY is pulling at CASEY's arm like a small toddler, she turns and jokes with him.)

CASEY: Just cause you is from Barking!

BILLY: I've.

CASEY:

BILLY: I've taken...

CASEY: Taken...

BILLY: Taken on...

CASEY: Taken on board...

BILLY: All…

CASEY: All that I said…

BILLY: Yeah!

CASEY: The life coach I recommended – he is helping you yeah?

BILLY: He knows…

CASEY: His stuff?

BILLY: Man…

CASEY: You are owning the traits?

BILLY: John/

CASEY: Charles/

BILLY: Clyde/

CASEY: Best/

BILLY: Rio and his work in the community innit!

CASEY: Thierry?

BILLY: Gazza: the childhood!

CASEY: Don't spend too much time on him…

BILLY: Nah bwai…

CASEY: Mental health issues and orange!

BILLY:

CASEY: You are the club's top striker and you are special and you are loved.

BILLY: I AM…

CASEY: DESERVING OF/

BILLY: LOVE…

CASEY: Glad you signed with me?

BILLY: Well/ happy

CASEY: Your old agent, Lenny Baxter…did nothing for you and your contract finished.

BILLY: My brother is next door, he's still got his tag and the curfew, but he is here!

(Big BILLY smile. CASEY and all, to us. FATIMA busy with hospitality.)

CASEY: The photographers didn't know quite what to do/

FRANK: Vol-au-vents?

JOEY: Barely touched the sides

FRANK: Some disabled fans/

(WOMAN IN WHEELCHAIR goes across the stage.)

CASEY: Had been wheeled in just for the/

TONY: So cynical!

CASEY: I wanted a chair from the boardroom, and I had asked Fatima/

FRANK: The old chairman's secretary, a juicy woman who had crossed a lot of lines, to get/

FATIMA: You know I can't talk about this…

(The scene. FATIMA holding the chair, CASEY smiles.)

FATIMA: Ok?

CASEY: Don't let Anthony get to you this evening…push those buttons…

FATIMA: Sorry but I am a professional and/

CASEY: No longer the mistress…

FATIMA:

CASEY: His wife tried to top herself again…

FATIMA: When?

CASEY: Linda found out he was carrying on again, and err after all the promises, more than she could take. Crazy/

FATIMA: Linda!

(FATIMA sits down visibly wounded.)

CASEY: So Casey was going to stand on this…

(She looks at the chair, which FATIMA is now seated on, FATIMA gets up. To us.) The crowd would look at her/

TONY: In yer dreams…

CASEY: I had written the speech myself and/

(The scene, LIANNE moves forward.)

LIANNE: If I go home right, they will only get another girl to help out at the players' private party and well…

CASEY: Put your fucking clothes on!

LIANNE: I can't see what I am doing that's wrong…

CASEY: Put your clothes on now…

LIANNE: Are you scared of sex or something?

CASEY: Do you advertise on the internet?

LIANNE: No, my mate gets me the gigs…

CASEY: You sure you not one of those girls, offering herself to be spit-roasted, blogging about the nicest cock at Reading and Orlando Bloom?

LIANNE: You got the wrong Lianne from Buckhurst Hill!

CASEY: Look I know it's your…profession, but this is no longer/

(To us.)

TONY: The way things are around here!

(Checking her phone. CASEY to us.)

CASEY: Michel had suddenly gone quiet, so I had to send/

(The scene, MICHEL in Spain, sitting in the sun, very Thierry.)

MICHEL: 'You are so exquisitely beautiful and you were never in a commercial? *(Beat.)* There's no bestseller, yet you've got such a marketable story, come and be my player and then join me here please!'

(To us.)

CASEY: I knew I had to surround myself with people…men, that I felt comfortable with, oh yeah that was tip number/

(The scene. BILLY steps forward.)

BILLY: My…brother…bro/

(JOEY enters.)

BILLY: *(Pointing to his brother.)* Facebook/

CASEY: After all these years…must be hugely/ rewarding…

JOEY: Finally, at fucking last, our own international tycoon…

CASEY: So the fans are very happy?

JOEY: Well…a state-of-the-art stadium right!

CASEY: Champions League…

JOEY: Much better…than the/

CASEY: Not so worthy World Cup!

JOEY: Yeah…

CASEY: More bleedin foreigners, with names you can't pronounce…

JOEY: Let's ave some…

CASEY: A new manager?

JOEY: Look, whatever it takes!

(Silence, she moves him away from the crowd.)

JOEY: Me and Billy Boy we had the same mum, but different dads, so that is why/

CASEY: Up and down the country, coming home covered in blood, bricks through coaches just for a laugh?

JOEY: Singing songs/

CASEY: To the Northerners...

JOEY: *(Singing.)* does the social know you're here...

CASEY: *(Singing.)* We pay your benefits...

(Silence.)

JOEY: And if me or any of my mates finished up inside, well we always made sure, that the kids of the blokes in prison always had the propa trainers...the propa gear on at school...

CASEY: Can't have the kids looking pikey...

JOEY: Just cause their old man's inside...

CASEY: Nah...

JOEY: If I am with Billy like...well he don't get trouble now, you know if I am with him in a club...well people used to come up to him/

CASEY: Average football fan is on about what...

JOEY: Eighteen grand a year...

CASEY: Glad he signed with me?

(LIANNE approaches again, CASEY is distracted and turns to LIANNE.)

CASEY: This is an important night for this club, an important night for...

LIANNE: Gonna tell me next that the game is all about the comfort of social habit and a worldwide need for tribal ritual and worship, within the parameters of rampant global capitalism...right?

CASEY: Walking up the road to the stadium with the men, the manor suddenly injected with life, the colours and the community…the dog shit miraculously no longer there… the poverty scrubbed away for a… *(Thinking.)* Suddenly a…

(A cheer from the crowd.)

LIANNE: Beauty!

CASEY: The racial tension not so important, although the lone black fan…

(We see a man being spat on.)

LIANNE:

CASEY: Ah the hormonal excitement, good old geezer glamour and the belonging, to feel connected, have some sort of religious experience…

LIANNE: To be able to talk about something the blokes were talking about?

(The fans are buzzing.)

CASEY: Standing on the North Bank with me dad and brothers, hearing the men swearing, and stab em…go on stab em…comrade tales of spitting in the pies, whilst at work on the production line for Fray Bentos…

LIANNE:

(Big beat. Money floods the stage, to us.)

CASEY: After/

FRANK: Hillsborough!

CASEY: *(Upbeat.)* Italia '90…

TONY: Renewed national interest in our national game!

JOEY: Caged fans/

CASEY: Football has/

FRANK: Some fit and proper people/

MICHEL: A growing hatred of the satellite faith?

TONY: The chairmen of the major clubs/

FRANK: The FA have been consistently helpful/

CASEY: A few blokes have become/

TONY: Loaded as a result of that early Nineties split/

CASEY: The more coverage/

BILLY: The more coins…

MICHEL: Now the scrutiny?

CASEY: Football cannot return to what it once was!

TONY: *(To CASEY.)* You are still onto a winner!

MICHEL: Still pocketing from, the Premiership…fiasco/

BILLY: Everyone's in debt blood…

CASEY: Derby spent loads…

FRANK: A soft loan…

BILLY: Liverpool, forty million quid each year…

TONY: Interest to the banks…

BILLY: Chelsea…

CASEY: Over seven hundred million/

BILLY: Man Utd. owe/

TONY: Even though they do get their money from/

CASEY: Sky's the limit, and have/

TONY: Bigger gate receipts and having a global…

CASEY: Brand/

BILLY: Cause everything costs a lot in this game…yeah!

CASEY: Cause/

BILLY: *(Beat, he affirms.)* To not risk, is to not win. I is seen all over the world...me give a lot of peeps pleasure...

JOEY: Two and half billion Premiership debts...cor that's a fucking lot!

FRANK: Stop trying to teach them –

MICHEL: What they already know!

(MICHEL now back in Spain, just out of the shower, still a bit wet, checking his phone.)

MICHEL: She starts her speech and I am in a hotel room in Andalucia, walking out, drying off, leaning on the balcony, another text, another Casey Layton email...and I decide to...

(He gets out his phone.)

CASEY:

MICHEL: The major players take up their starting positions... and Layton wants people to listen...listen up!

(The Scene. FRANK comes forward, CASEY has to shout, lots of cameras.)

CASEY: Today my company finally organized and facilitated a major deal with Frank Wong, for him to take over as chairman of this club.

(To us.)

FRANK: She made a couple of million, for just getting two men together. Saving the old chairman's life...stopping Ray salt of the earth Cook from hanging himself!

(The scene. FRANK coughs.)

CASEY: This footballing institution, the lifeblood and centre of our community, which is part of my very soul, is moving forward, and is now creating a new/

FRANK: Legacy, for all of us to be a part of...

(To us.)

MICHEL: Asking myself do I really want to get into all of this…

(The scene.)

CASEY: Now I know many of you…have had difficulties in the not so distant past…with this club being owned by a foreign investor and this being a family club…

However the world is changing, football has changed and we all need to finally move on. We cannot be left behind. The word is evolution…global competitive evolution and we need to be able to seriously compete and win, in a changing world/

BILLY: Change is exciting!

CASEY: Exactly Billy…exactly/

(JOEY even louder than his brother.)

JOEY: Champions League one day...

CASEY: I can see it and feel it and fifty million immediately to spend in the next transfer window…this little of slice of London is going global…going global big time…and into the Premiership!

(MICHEL speaks to us.)

MICHEL: Who would really want to be part of all this!

(The scene, various angles.)

CASEY: Asia as we all know is the growing economy even in these financially challenging times, middle-class parents who have their eye on the ball are aware that China is the future and where their children's futures reside. Mothers in Primrose Hill already teaching their kiddies Mandarin, cause they seriously know that these are the people we are daily going to be communicating with, doing our daily business with in a very short time, and why can't mothers in other areas follow suit and do the same eh? Do the same, and get our kids to learn the language too? We have to re-programme ourselves to be adaptable now, but coming as always from the cockney heart. Again we have to welcome and embrace/

FRANK: Change!

CASEY: People have notions in business that you have to trample over everyone! But an entrepreneur like Frankie Wong creates an environment, a club where ideas can be explored and where everyone's contribution is valued.

FRANK:

CASEY: So we let go of the stories that kept us stuck and we all move on together.

FRANK: Together/

CASEY: We are going to be open about our new strategies but Rome wasn't built in a day and your loyalty, and your patience are going to be required and rewarded as we build up this new structure, invest in our neglected academy and promote this new responsible foundation. We have the enthusiasm and I hope you all have too…So will you join me and/

FRANK: Just call me Frankie yeah!

CASEY: The corruption that is destroying our game, will not be tolerated at this club/

JOEY: What about us?

CASEY: Even though times are hard for many of our fans/

FRANK: Casey…

(ANTHONY enters, stands in front of CASEY. FATIMA watching from a distance.)

TONY: She's in a bad way, on this drip, loads of machines… she's sleeping all the time, and she woke up to tell me,

38

she… Linda's a mother, soon to be a grandmother again, a bloody good woman… I promise I will get you all where you want to be. I have never failed you, I just didn't have the right amount money to spend, but now I have; now I have and I am your manager, your local boy that will take you into the next chapter. I love this club, I love my players, and I love you all…

FRANK: *(Walking over to TONY.)* We are all with you, at this difficult time.

TONY: That means everything to me!

FRANK: *(Holding out his hand.)* The gaffer!

TONY: *(Shaking FRANK's hand.)* Cheers boss.

(Tears in his eyes, to everyone.) Thank you!

(To us.)

MICHEL: She phoned me.

(The scene. CASEY on her phone to Spain; TONY, FRANK and the lads, enjoying a joke.)

CASEY: I want to be your agent and I need you here at my club.

MICHEL: Why?

CASEY: You will bring maturity…stability to the team and… hopefully some *consistent* touches of genius.

MICHEL: So you really have cut out the booze and coke and random sex?

CASEY: I have had some…

MICHEL: Expensive therapy in expensive places?

CASEY: Frank and Anthony Whitechapel are bonding!

MICHEL: You want to represent me…

CASEY: Nobody else wants to Michel!

(MICHEL to us.)

MICHEL: I downloaded and signed her contract. Sent it back to her, via the hotel reception. Casey was my agent and I would soon have a job. I went to sleep and she was in my, in my…dream.

CASEY: EARLY OCTOBER, sixteen points and a lacklustre draw at Doncaster Rovers!

TONY: Fuck!

CASEY: I had delivered everything and Frank had got all he had initially/

FRANK: Wished for?

CASEY: However he appeared to not be keeping his promise to me. My number one plan was still to get Tony/

TONY: The sack!

CASEY: And to put in place a new manager, this however didn't seem to be on Frank's agenda anymore. *(Beat.)* Because Frankie and myself had always had a bit of sexual/

FRANK: She would do anything!

JOEY: *(Looking at LAYTON.)* Wouldn't mind a go!

TONY: Casey was daily affirming the new person she wanted to become – tip number…

ALL: WHAT A LOAD OF BOLLOCKS!

CASEY: The dynamics were hard; I was finding communication difficult…

FRANK: Not like when we first met…

JOEY: *(Sexy voice.) Action* replay.

(The scene, FRANK's hotel. CASEY and FRANK have been drinking, up close and personal, hotel music plays.)

CASEY: I don't believe that all the money is going out of England…

FRANK: No English jobs for English boys…

CASEY: London is thriving with talent and the major four are in every primary school sniffing out the kids, so the local children are getting chances, even if there are limited spaces for them to play…

FRANK: So you will buy me footballers from anywhere I want?

CASEY: This is the most exciting time in history/

FRANK: I just want a team that wins…I just want, need to be in The Premiership/

CASEY: Then I am your woman; I know who wants to sell.

FRANK: Get your finders fee/

CASEY: It's not just about money.

(FRANK watches her.)

FRANK: Anyone waiting up for you?

CASEY: Life long fear of commitment me…

FRANK: Compliments your commitment to a higher cause?

BOTH: Football!

CASEY: I have always wanted a job where I had to take it on the chin, face it like a man/

FRANK: Prove to them that you have bigger balls than the Russian…

CASEY: And that scares a lot of men!

FRANK: Let's go to my room…

CASEY: Will a football club, be the biggest present you ever bought for yourself?

FRANK: Nearly the biggest!

CASEY: Can I be the one to wrap it for you then…

FRANK: Fish and chips…

CASEY: English/

FRANK: Batter…

(CASEY turning quickly to us.)

CASEY: Frank once flew two hundred of his friends from Tokyo to LA – with all the cabin crew – even the male pilot – completely naked!

FRANK: This is all just from one perspective!

TONY: Mid-October and a spectacular win for us at Leicester City

MICHEL: And I was starting to get her phone calls…texts…she needed me…it was seven o'clock, the following morning…

(London/Spain.)

MICHEL: What do I want to earn a week?

CASEY: Maybe you would like to buy some property, have a look at tax planning investments?

MICHEL: *(Sleepy.)* Charitable gifting…

CASEY: Launching perhaps a…ethical clothing company?

(Silence.)

CASEY: It's good to hear your voice…

MICHEL: Really?

(He laughs, she laughs. A manuscript is delivered to CASEY, she puts down the phone, reading. To us.)

MICHEL: And she then rings me back and suddenly rants at me down the/

FRANK: Casey was being unprofessional…

MICHEL: Layton trusted me!

(The scene. CASEY reading a manuscript. We see TONY collecting money from around the ground, lots and lots of brown envelopes.)

CASEY: You know how much Whitechapel made out of the Terry Fisher deal?

MICHEL: About fifty thousand quid.

CASEY: What a…

MICHEL: Everyone knows what he's like, many take bungs and you also take your cut. So you really want to nail him?

CASEY: Whitechapel bought Palmer for two point four million and only brought him on six times, because he had a cartilage problem.

MICHEL: Although Palmer continued to rave all night and run a marathon! Whitechapel then sold Palmer for an undisclosed fee, as always, no questions please!

CASEY: Fucking…

MICHEL: The sacking culture forces managers to act…

CASEY: Criminally?

(To us.)

CASEY: I had to see Frank. Early November and/

TONY: A wonderful win against Barnsley!

CASEY: Twenty-nine points and…alright I was blinded by my mission…and the end would justify the means…

JOEY: *(To CASEY.)* You alright?

(The scene, FRANK is watching football, lusting after MESSI.)

CASEY: Could get him here. *(Looking at Argentina's finest on the television.)* Couple of year's time, have an in…

(FRANK looks at her, laughs, she is being completely serious.)

FRANK: Who else can you attract?

CASEY: Say a name…

FRANK:

CASEY: Go on say a name…

FRANK: At Arsenal…

CASEY: It all could happen y'know…

FRANK: We need to get some Premiership players on loan, for after Christmas…that is the priority!

CASEY: Don't worry about a thing…

FRANK:

(She goes to leave and then decides against it.)

CASEY: But Frank…English managers/

FRANK: English Managers can't win the Premiership… England… Englishness isn't a winning mentality anymore/

CASEY:

FRANK: Weak Casey…weak!

(Beat, she rests on his desk.)

CASEY: Alright…football is not predictable/

FRANK: Epicuric/

CASEY: Don't think that's a word!

FRANK: Lacking in competition?

CASEY: But it is about product, attracting the finest possible product and/

FRANK: You keep telling me that you can give me good product…

CASEY: One hundred per cent!

FRANK: So you don't think the Emirates is an empty architectural wonder, funded by cheating Arabs?

CASEY: I know that you can provide the resources…

FRANK: We scored four goals on Saturday; we are doing well in the FA Cup. Hated your speech by the way...

CASEY: We can achieve everything here together. However, nobody...special wants to play and work with Whitechapel, and Anthony will try to shaft us, in any way he can, and he needs to go...

FRANK: Casey you just facilitated the initial meet.

CASEY: It was a bit more, than just getting you and Ray Cook to drink tea in The Landmark Hotel!

FRANK: Was it?

CASEY: Remember us and the consortium all watching Barcelona together?

FRANK: And you remember that you are not the chairman, or on the board even...ok so you have a five per cent share option...you are an agent, that is all you are Casey!

CASEY: Anthony Whitechapel will rip us off. Like he did before...just like he did to the old owners...

FRANK: Where is the proof...?

CASEY: My friend...the journalist...

FRANK: Whose book was never published...?

CASEY: But other books are out there in print and there was a police investigation...they searched Anthony's house!

FRANK: Nothing was found...

CASEY: But what if something is very close to being found, look this QC I met...

FRANK: He thinks Whitechapel could eventually go to jail?

CASEY: And what if there then is a major delve into finances at this club. We don't want any hint of scandal here do we? Frankie...

(Silence.)

FRANK: I need it in black and white!

(MICHEL to us.)

MICHEL: Anyone could be agent, when Casey first started out see!

(CASEY on her phone and walking around the club, major activity – all involved. CASEY to us.)

CASEY: Thirty-two points, off to find Fatima, make a quick call to a Premiership manager, and tweet a rumour about an unhappy lad at a club in North London.

MICHEL: It was the game, not playing a straight one was endemic, wasn't it Casey?

CASEY: Thought you were on my side?

(The scene segues into team training, lots of skill. CASEY watching.)

FATIMA: Why have you injuncted me?

TONY: It was the lawyer's call.

FATIMA: You had no say in the matter?

TONY: I told them you were a clever girl and wouldn't utter a word!

FATIMA: I am excellent at my job yeah, and our last chairman respected me and having an attractive Asian woman as PA to the chairman, makes you all look very good!

TONY: *(Direct.)* Frank won't sack you.

FATIMA:

TONY: Had a dream about the play offs last night…

FATIMA: Fuck you…

(TONY begins to walk away.)

TONY: Making love in the Premier Inn

(She shouts after him.)

FATIMA: You then promising as always to leave Linda. I will leave her…I will, I give you my word… I will…

TONY: *(Returning.)* Sorry!

FATIMA: Who is your new mistress?

TONY: It was like a…spiritual moment…

FATIMA: Who is she? Who the fuck is she Tony?

TONY: You told me right…that I opened you up to the stars/

FATIMA: We drank too much…

TONY: Look I've got to go and see Frank and err…

FATIMA: I lie in bed in the mornings and I plan my day…and my tasks for the day are breaking my mad addiction to Anthony Whitechapel/

TONY: *(To his player.)* Fuck's sake Billy, concentrate! I hear you.

(He starts to leave.)

FATIMA: And you run away…go on, off you go…not going there…because to go there would sacrifice the ego…the man, the myth…

TONY: *(Returning.)* You see me as a loser and you're my saviour/

FATIMA: Growing up in the school of hard fucking knocks…

TONY: My dad right, don't show any emotion, or I will beat the shit out of you…

FATIMA: A mummy who left…

TONY: I call your phone just to hear your voice/

FATIMA: I can't be one of nine…I have to be number one and you made your choice!

TONY: This is not an easy time for me/

(He gets very upset, to us.)

CASEY: And it went on and on and it was a game, I had been in many many times/

MICHEL: Yeah!

(The scene, everyone looks at their watches.)

TONY: I still have the pictures of you on my phone!

FATIMA: This is sick...

(Suddenly everyone has perked up.)

FATIMA: You won't keep getting away with all of this...they will get you one day...someone will get you/

TONY: Sooner rather than later I hope.

FATIMA: In time a woman will come along – who you genuinely want to evolve for and when your inadequate heart breaks and you really start to crumble/

TONY: She came along alright...

(He walks away, the team follows. CASEY walks into the scene.)

FATIMA: *(Holding back the tears.)* Sorry, sorry...yeah...hope we win again this weekend...it's all about the winning... I spoke to Casey Layton about Linda... I thought Casey was full of shit...but I think she wants to be my friend...be on my/

CASEY: Anthony can't really love anyone.

FATIMA: Because ultimately he believes they will always abandon him, so he abandons them first...

CASEY: And he's a narcissist.

FATIMA: *(Wiping her eyes.)* Equal opportunities Casey eh...

CASEY: *(Trying to comfort her.)* Let me give you a...

FATIMA: I just want to keep my job!

CASEY: If you do need to talk...

FIT AND PROPER PEOPLE

FATIMA:

> *(CASEY on her phone, to us.)*

CASEY: So I was building up my hand, slowly slotting stuff into place.

FRANK: Thirty-three points, moving up the table.

MICHEL: Ignoring her calls. She would never leave the great English game.

CASEY: And be your wife in Africa?

FRANK: Thirty-four points.

TONY: Suddenly in a play off position!

CASEY: Eventually a softer, more feminine voicemail, prompted Michel to call me back.

> *(The scene, MICHEL in SPAIN and in the shade reading. CASEY leaves her flat, she is in a cab, checks her passport.)*

CASEY: Tony didn't allow any other agents a look-in/

MICHEL: Because him and Lenny Baxter were mates in it together and seriously creaming money in from infinite sides. If you really want a player, sod the cost, sod everything!

CASEY: Tony sacked Jenny in marketing who was on a pathetic fifteen grand per year and/

MICHEL: Tripled the salary and gave the job to his cousin. What's new…it's football…it's the world as we know it Casey Layton…?

CASEY: Yet he still has unconditional footballing love, and this is going to be harder than I ever imagined…

MICHEL: Women can never deliver on the pitch…that's why they are treated like they are.

CASEY: I have to follow up these leads.

(CASEY is at Heathrow, walking to her gate.)

MICHEL: Casey you have hardly been pure/

CASEY: What have you been doing today?

MICHEL: Head full of memories…

CASEY: Transforming a car park into a pitch for you and your friends!

Balls made from paper and string…

MICHEL: You want me to come and play in England, for *your* team next season and…

CASEY: Yes!

(CASEY is delayed at airport.)

CASEY: Shit!

(The scene, she is sitting reading the manuscript, MICHEL speaks to us. Images of Africa start to appear on the screen.)

MICHEL: The Europeans sailed to my beautiful continent –

(Taking back her ball, to us.)

CASEY: Bringing with them the bible, the cricket bat and of course the holy football.

MICHEL: These were the white man's precious gifts/

CASEY: The things to transform the/

MICHEL: Violent hungry savages into being honest decent Christian gentleman?

(The scene.)

CASEY: You want me to help you build the Michel Gbagbo Centre in the middle of your village, once you have quit playing?

(To us.)

FRANK: Another draw…

TONY: Ipswich Town! *(To FATIMA.)* Redbridge Travelodge?

(MICHEL phones CASEY. The scene.)

MICHEL: Why did you put the phone down on me?

CASEY: I didn't!

MICHEL: Why you going to Benin?

CASEY: Are you telepathic or something…

MICHEL: So what's your business out there?

(CASEY's phone bleeps, she looks at it.)

CASEY: Babe, my scout, the club's scout, Tommy Thomas/

MICHEL: Tony's best mate.

CASEY: Just called me. I paid him this retainer…to always bell me first/

MICHEL: Can you hear me?

(CASEY closes her phone, speaks again to us, footage of a very poor game being played by young African kids, MICHEL closes his phone.)

CASEY: It was fundamental that I built up the younger players at the club, shake up the apathy in the academy, invest in more new blood/

TONY: Secure all channels for the prime talent coming through.

CASEY: I was further exploiting an already corrupted market? Yes I was, and I *was* on a plane to a city in the Edo State of Nigeria. Up above the clouds, I could feel some presence surrounding me, I was either deluded or something higher was indeed guiding me now…you know the feeling?

TONY: *(On his phone.)* Is she taking the piss?

CASEY: It was hot. *(Beat.)*

FRANK: She was met at the airport, by a man called Yoann and they drove for a shaky, sticky two hours. Our player, Razak, lived in a small traditional village/

(TOMMY/JOEY hungover comes and stands next to CASEY, footage fades. To us.)

TOMMY: A shack, with just about running water. I mean, I get to see every conceivable kind of shit hole, in my line of work.

CASEY: The potential world-class talent was living with his devoted grandfather.

(RAZAK shows off his skills.)

TOMMY: Razak didn't speak English; well he could hardly speak anything at all. Although a bit old at sixteen, Razak was the real deal. He had bleedin' everything. Hadn't been this fired up since I first saw Jermaine, many moons ago. Where had Razak been fucking hiding?

CASEY: Having watched the footage Tommy had sent me, I was about to see the kid play in the flesh. After the match, I spoke quietly to Mouftaou/

TOMMY: Grandad!

(The scene. Silence, MOUFTAOU/MICHEL thinks. MOUFTAOU's new wife/FRANK sits in the background, skinning a chicken. The entire village is watching the barefoot boy do his after the game thing.)

MOUFT: We had someone working on behalf of Tottenham Hotspur, here just the other day, saying exactly the same/

TOMMY: Making similar noises!

MOUFT: You want to take him to England?

CASEY: A year in our academy for starters.

MOUFT: Where will he live?

CASEY: He can stay with a family I know, great friends of
     mine. A wonderful woman, known her since I was a child
     myself.

MOUFT: Who will pay for all of this?

CASEY: He will be on a small wage, and his rent and meals
     will all be looked after by my company. If he works hard,
     he could end up as you know being signed by the club,
     and then possibly straight into first team football and
     obviously The Premiership. It could be as quick and simple
     as all that. The financial rewards could be huge.

TOMMY: Life-changing, transform this village, your
     community, transform just about everything/

MOUFT: We are not the Congo; we do get Sky in this country.

TOMMY: Now Mouftaou you liked the idea of Razak, staying
     with you, staying at the academy set up by err... Being
     able to keep a close eye on him, but you have got to let
     him go and have a crack at his dream...ain't yer?

MOUFT: He just wants to play football; he isn't a greedy child.

TOMMY: He's got ambition; the kid wants it all...

MOUFT: Can you/

CASEY: Can I what?

(MOUFTAOU thinks, they wait.)

MOUFT: Nobody from Benin has ever reached further than
     second division French football, what makes you think
     Razak could do any different?

TOMMY: Stephane Sessegnon?

MOUFT: Nobody has really heard of our country, our players
     don't know people who are influential in the game...

CASEY: Well Razak knows me now, doesn't he?

(MOUFTAOU looks at her.)

GEORGIA FITCH

MOUFT: You hear about all this stuff going on back in
England, young…black players are targets I think!

CASEY: That's just stories that sell cheap newspapers, stuff you
can read about on the internet.

TOMMY: Stir up things, push deals through, everyone hates
Ashley!

MOUFT: I need to be sure that he will be alright!

CASEY: Razak would sign a contract with me, making him
initially my player for two years. I will take fifteen per cent
of his earnings, once he was, is signed, but up until then, I
will work for him for free.

MOUFT: Do you have children?

CASEY: My players are my sons.

TOMMY: Too right.

CASEY: Razak is a credit to you.

(More silence.)

MOUFT: The man from Spurs, offered to buy him his own flat,
in Turnpike Lane.

TOMMY: Look…

MOUFT: Driving lessons and a run around little motor…

CASEY: I will see what I can do!

MOUFT: Perhaps even an advance…on the major deal…

CASEY: Don't push your luck…alright/

TOMMY: Grandad!

*(CASEY picks up her phone, moves across the stage, back in England,
Heathrow to the club, speaking to us.)*

CASEY: So save money at all costs, and eat regularly, was…

Tips not important to me anymore…

FRANK: Thirty-six points and…

TONY: Still in the top six!

(The team enters, frantic.)

CASEY: And things had started to well and truly kick off and/

MICHEL: As she landed back in the UK, *(Mocking.)* again trying to do stuff the right way, again/

CASEY: I was coming up against it all/

BILLY: Guns!

(BILLY has a shooter in his hands.)

JOEY: *(Taking it from BILLY.)* Fifteen-year-old baby mothers /

FRANK: Players!!!

MICHEL: Who had that impulse, that cellular memory/

TONY: Physical need in the body, to score/

JOEY: Win and have what they want at any fucking cost/

MICHEL: Yet lacking the wiring in the brain, to stop/

JOEY: They shouldn't really be held up as role models…

CASEY: All phone calls waiting to be quickly returned!

(To MICHEL, The scene, football chaos in background.)

CASEY: Sorry did I cut you off?

MICHEL: About three days ago!

CASEY: Sean Kelly/

MICHEL: From Norris Green/

CASEY: This one's really young…

MICHEL: So will the local gangsters really kill his mother this time?

CASEY: Over a scally…slag?

MICHEL: Slightly a bit less important…than him playing down south!

CASEY: Control the footballer, control the forgotten city!

MICHEL: Was you trying to get him at your club too?

(Beat, a gunshot is heard.)

CASEY: Has my Jerome Johnson ever raped a woman?

MICHEL: You also look after Jerome?

CASEY: Tell me…

MICHEL: I don't know Casey… I don't…

CASEY: Razak joined the academy, Tommy Thomas brought him home. He signed with me and seemed to be alright.

(TOMMY moves forward again hungover.)

TOMMY: Granddad was given a couple of grand, out of Casey's personal account. *(Beat.)* There was no current Director of Football at the club, the only person, apart from the head of the club's not so thriving academy, who needed to be consulted, was in fact Anthony. *(Beat.)* Frank had a photo of Layton, via me, via Anthony's top drawer – that had landed on his desk…

(TOMMY gives the photo to FRANK, FRANK looks at it, both share a laugh. CASEY closes her phone. The scene. FRANK watches more football and switches to a different game, the photo remains on the table, CASEY looks at it.)

FRANK: Miss Wet Tit Shirt – 1983!

CASEY: Nice…

FRANK: Posted through my door…

CASEY: Clever Tony…

FRANK: When are you going to lighten up Casey Layton… when did you lose your sense of humour? *(Looking again at the photo.)* Pert knockers back then…

CASEY: Getting everything in place for you Frank, for after Christmas and then next season. Lots of Premiership players interested in being on loan here, and I will soon be representing every footballer at this club.

(She produces a newspaper article from her bag, turns off the telly, sits on his desk.)

CASEY: Another report is out/

FRANK: I don't need to read it...

CASEY: Frank!

FRANK: It's going to be more droning on about sharing earnings...wealth redistribution...dividing the revenue from the television and sponsorship deals, between the twenty teams in the Premiership, like the good old days...

CASEY: I think you should read it...

FRANK: Quotas of English players in line-ups and putting limits on the size of squads? Training the nation's children, making them feel alright about keeping the ball... I know how it goes...

Your country's national footballing infrastructure is way behind the rest of Europe; they can't even deal with that...

CASEY: Trying to challenge the game on issues that are in the public interest/

FRANK: Who owns your football clubs/

CASEY: Well it isn't the British!

FRANK: Winning is the only thing of any interest to any public anywhere in the world...

CASEY: The fans, the real people around here are broke and they aren't that happy with the price of things!

FRANK: They can still get credit...or you can just ignore their emails.

(Pause.)

CASEY: Look, do you want me to speak to the fans on your behalf? I mean they do sort of trust me Frank, what with being local and all that...

FRANK: I am managing to service the fucking debt, what else could your community, our fans ask for?

(He switches the telly back on. She tries yet again to engage him in debate.)

FRANK: Your government let me in, we both will be alright. They have to do these things now and again Casey... thought they had enough to worry about, covering their own backs...

CASEY: Wanting the major clubs to share a bit of their earnings...create a slightly more level playing field, can only be a good thing for us, surely a realistic option for the club, as we go into that league...before we all go into/

FRANK: You are fucking joking?

CASEY: We want to reassure our fans that everything is going to be alright don't we?

FRANK: We have thirty-nine points, Whitechapel is up for manager of the month...

CASEY: I found a manager, he is Italian, an icon, was an amazing player, would make a fantastic/

FRANK: No, concentrate on the squad... Gbagbo?

CASEY: I can read your mind!

FRANK: Off you go...

(CASEY leaves, she returns.)

CASEY: Translator's fees, for Scottish players...

FRANK: I don't want to hear about what Tony supposedly did, two fucking years ago...

CASEY: When Ray Cook was in Marbella… Whitechapel/

FRANK: You are being paid, to find me talent. Lure players from lesser clubs/

CASEY: Those who are skint/

FRANK: Those who perhaps/

CASEY: Are suddenly finding that all their best players are leaving – because the lads are only in it for the money, and they obviously want to play for clubs that pay the most. The fans then become disheartened, and attempt to do something else with their lives and the club eventually is propelled into administration…and the local community lose their jobs…

FRANK: Get the footballers I like interested/

CASEY: Gbagbo…

FRANK: Break their contracts if need be, get them down here, take your fifteen per cent and leave Anthony to me. Got that? Now fuck off!

CASEY:

(Silence. MICHEL rings CASEY, she is on the move again.)

MICHEL: I have been looking at flights…

CASEY: Got to email the Dutch clubs, Jerome needs to get out of England.

MICHEL: Has he expressed this to his own manager yet…

CASEY: His own manager advised it…

MICHEL: Incredible…

CASEY: Will bell you back.

(To us.)

CASEY: Off to find mistress Fatima and we get thrashed at fucking Millwall.

(The scene. TONY straight over to CASEY.)

TONY: Let's go out for dinner one night.

CASEY:

(Beat.)

TONY: I would genuinely like to spend some quality time with you.

CASEY: What to ensure that I will keep my mouth shut?

TONY: Casey, please…

CASEY: Some average high dining and a cab home, being your idea of fair exchange?

TONY: Somewhere in town and we could just chat outside of this…circus!

(He gives her a TONY smile.)

CASEY: You and me are ancient history Anthony, it's all in the past and I am not going to let you penetrate my business or my future/

TONY: You've got this radiance, it's magnetic…

CASEY: You look a mess!

TONY: Not an easy time at the moment…

CASEY: What do you dream about?

TONY: Playing Man Utd. and knocking that smile off Sir Alex's smug face… Tactics going round in your… Casey… Are you alright beautiful?

(Big big silence.)

TONY: You nearly married a once-good footballer I heard/

(LIANNE walks across the stage, past CASEY. LIANNE is in a world of her own.)

CASEY: What is she doing here?

TONY: Who you talking about?

(CASEY watching LIANNE fade/leave the stage. Silence.)

TONY: My kids are well worried about their mum.

CASEY: And it still feels like fucking yesterday to me…can still taste it…smell it…seventy grand on therapy…and I am still wanting to throw up!

(He looks at her.)

TONY: I want to keep my job at this club Casey. Football managing is the thing I do best.

CASEY: Strong in the game…

TONY: I never intended to hurt you darling, you just got caught up in all the…and I wanted to trace you…I tried to find you…the boys made me promise…blackmailed me, to never see you again!

CASEY: Liar.

TONY: All I wanted…all my life…the only thing I have ever ever wanted was see…was for people to like me…

CASEY: You always bring everything back to you…

TONY: I am so proud of my girl…everything you have achieved…

CASEY: I hate you.

TONY: Don't get so into being this hard ball-breaking bitch, that you shut yourself off from all love, and don't you lose yer basic compassion mate, because you are still that little girl to me, underneath all of this…still my…

(He studies her body.)

I know who you really are and what you want and what you need and… I *know* what a lifetime of shit and guilt feels like…

(She moves away.)

CASEY: Freedom Tony, oblivion Tony, *(In his face.)* winning Tony…the thing that football tries to take us all to in a quick ninety minutes, that's what I want now mate!

TONY: The world wants release babe…

CASEY: That feeling *you* get from spending a shed load of other people's money, driving the fastest motor, a filthy shag, with an exotic woman/

TONY: Trying to make myself feel good…

(He goes to walk away.)

CASEY: That place you get to, where nothing else matters, that space where there are no worries and no doubts and you feel safe and certain and you can melt into it all and everything is perfect and goal, you did it, you got there…

TONY: Winning…yeah, winning…

CASEY: Space less and timeless…

TONY: The god bit in our brains…

CASEY: Where nothing can touch you, nothing can hurt you anymore!

TONY: Look…

CASEY: My game plan is just a bit more evolved than yours these days see…

TONY: The people in my fucking head…the grief, the everyday constant stress.

CASEY: You wanted the job, you thought you were man enough to do it, steer the ship. All your choice.

TONY: You have profited out of deals…

CASEY: Another book is coming out soon…

TONY: Some left wing, unfunny, bland middle-class writer… writing another forgettable book about my supposed little secrets…but secrets is what makes the world go around

CASEY: How dare you...

TONY: Sorry, alright, sorry!

CASEY: You're a dying cartoon/

TONY: We always get riled by the things we see in others don't we, that we haven't admitted to ourselves...that we are like that too...

CASEY: So what's the latest on the tax evasion case?

(He goes to walk away, then stops.)

TONY: Little presents to ourselves, fat cunts in Spain, who are well past their sell by date, yet can still go all night, making you feel not so old and desperate...little treats/

CASEY: Send Linda my love.

TONY: I don't want a war. Please Casey; I don't want a bloody war!

I NEVER EVER WANTED A WAR WITH YOU!

CASEY: Are you threatening me?

TONY: Agents have wrecked the game, but you are going way too far/

CASEY: Woman...

(To us. CASEY and MICHEL step forward.)

CASEY: Bit upset, but eh...no time for feelings and on with the job!

MICHEL: Another phone call from Casey, where we play:

CASEY: Who has had the hardest life!

(The scene, more phone deals, more reassuring players, and more football on the television.)

MICHEL: I came to Hackney at eleven and it was horrible.

CASEY: Look I do want you to come over, meet Frank face to face, I think you could swing it…sorry I've been distracted!

MICHEL: The violence!

(CASEY looks at her watch, gets out her iPad.)

CASEY: We will be in The Premiership.

MICHEL: The names and the constant insults.

CASEY: *(Reading her emails.)* My community went hungry…my community today still is hungry for some sort of…

MICHEL: Who is your community Casey… Don't kid me… You are still a selfish woman…with an horrific ego/

(To us.)

MICHEL: I obviously phrased it slightly kinder than that…

(The scene.)

CASEY: You are important to me…

(To us.)

CASEY: I THINK I KNOW WHAT I AM/

(The scene.)

MICHEL: Don't try and make me into your other men.

(CASEY reads her emails, multi-tasking yet again. Activity around the ground. To us.)

JOEY: *(Looking at BILLY.)* Human shit magnets…

TONY: People in this game… Holiday Inn Fatima?

CASEY: A happy man marries the girl he loves, but a happier man loves the girl he marries…

MICHEL: If you are digging a pit for your enemy, don't make it too deep, for you may fall into it.

CASEY: Up to my eyes in this shit/

TONY: Run-up to Christmas/

FRANK: And stuck at thirty-nine points...

(Silence. The scene, lonely CASEY.)

MICHEL: Why can't you let this Anthony Whitechapel thing go?

CASEY: Look the club, I…I am offering you a really good deal. I will email you the details again, and we will sit down and talk about your centre. But babe, remember Frank turns on a sixpence, so we need to move fast. When's your flight darling?

TONY: I told Frank, the fat cunt in Spain, wasn't a great idea!

(FRANK continues to watch the telly. CASEY looks at her phone, looks at FRANK. The team start to play a lot of football again. A woman in a wheelchair is wheeled into the club. To us.)

CASEY: I'd been giving the ball away far too much, would have to come out fighting in the second half.

TONY: Following a bender at Chinawhites, Barking's finest scored a fantastic late winner for us on Boxing Day!

(The scene.)

BILLY: BILLY WILLIAMS BWAI, BILLY WILLIAMS BWAI, BILLY WILLIAMS BWAI!

JOEY: OUT OF THIS FUCKING WORLD!

BILLY: Casey hadn't been there for me!

FRANK: Forty-two points.

TONY: *(To CASEY.)* Third in the table!

(Half-time.)

(To us.)

CASEY: Following some New Year's Day scandal.

BILLY: Lies blood…

CASEY: MY EARS IN THE DRESSING ROOM/

JOEY: Her boy…

TONY: Billy Williams wasn't match fit!

CASEY: He had eventually gone on…

JOEY: For fifteen minutes in the reserves and/

BILLY: He punched me first man!

CASEY: Billy was becoming a huge/

TONY: Sandwich short, donkey…

BILLY: *(Taking a photo of himself.)* Dick!

CASEY: Suddenly I had to quickly focus on, prioritize the neglected sections/

FRANK: That contributed to her Getting Tony Out Master Plan. *(Beat.)*

TONY: Mid-January, forty-five points and we demolish Portsmouth!

ALL: Get in!

CASEY: Even though I was thinking about my need for fresh proof, in limbo Michel!

MICHEL: *(To CASEY.)* So Frank doesn't want me anymore?

FRANK: And Mr Wong's money…'where did it all come from?'… Not quite at this moment in time, ladies and gentlemen…

CASEY: For this was somewhat urgent…

(CASEY walks into the scene, a designer shop.)

Billy, myself and/

JOEY: Joey went shopping!

CASEY: Buying them both some new clothes…

(BILLY enters in a blingy new outfit, JOEY also tries on the latest labels, does a bit of a hip hop dance, walks like a generic bad man.)

CASEY: After the spree/

FRANK: She booked Billy in for some extra special healing/

TONY: Some fucking hippie, anger management…and we are supposed to believe what Layton says? Take her seriously?

FRANK: Williams was going to up his self-worth, energetically be transported back in the team.

MICHEL: Anything that worked, that had always been her mantra!

CASEY: Joey insisted on coming again too, and Billy wanted/

JOEY: His family there and Layton needed us fans innit!

(She closes her phone. The scene. CASEY, BILLY and JOEY seated. CRAIG; the Buddhist/healer/FRANK, dressed in bright orange, faces the trio. CRAIG is centred and calm.)

BILLY: You will be going back to Dagenham, if you don't pull yer fucking

TONY: socks up/

BILLY: If I could only start, If only I could start gaffer/ I'm the manager…not you alright, I pick the team…you got that? YOU GOT THAT BILLY BOY?/ I was the best scorer last season. Fan's player of the year innit?/ But this is this season/ And I am fit and you are not giving me a chance man/ You are not fucking fit and what have I told you… WHAT HAVE I TOLD YOU?/ BUT I AM NOT PLAYING… I am not… I am not!

CRAIG: Just concentrate on the breath Billy…

BILLY: I am from London, I am a fan, I is the player… who when they play…wears the number 23: best and fastest selling shirt…when a new kit is launched every season bwai…in the stadium shop, signed photos of me/ Fucking well done mate/ Gaffer/ Change your tune boy Billy…change your/ Gaffer/ you know why people hate

67

footballers, because they are rich, thick and part of the nig nog under class, just like/

CRAIG: Breathe…

BILLY: Chris and Luke…they fought each other on the pitch… when they were playing for the same team…but you bought them here and seem to love them…then there is Lewis…he kicked the shit out of a Paki, his words… HE'S A RACIST MAN, in the BNP… A… You brought him here that season too and you love and play him/ I help… me…it's me…it's just what I do, way I am made…well they lost their little way, and they need me…to help them all get back on track/ gaffer/ I save people Billy Boy/ I want to start gaffer… I want to start!/ Shut the fuck up! SHUT THE FUCK UP BITCH! *(Beat.)*

TONY: Tell me what you heard…

(They all sit in silence.)

BILLY: We going to do talking to the media, setting intentions and tings?

CASEY: One step at a time Billy Boy, one step at a/

CRAIG: *(Looking at his watch.)* Time…

(Silence.)

BILLY: Me bro wants a go like!

CRAIG: *(CASEY gives CRAIG some money.)* Roleplay, Joey.

CASEY: Whitechapel was stealing from the club, from Billy and the fans….

JOEY: But Whitechapel got an apology from The Old Bill…

CASEY:

JOEY: *(Looking at CRAIG.)* In your own time… Craig!

(JOEY and CRAIG take up their positions, on the floor. Cushions spread; Craig attempts to 'channel' ANTHONY WHITECHAPEL.)

JOEY: Scumbag fucking scum…

CRAIG & TONY: *(Soft.)* I don't know what you mean…

CRAIG: I…don't know what you…

JOEY: Don't take us as complete fools alright/

CRAIG: *(Building.)* Look this is all a bit… Japanese to me…

CASEY: Great!

JOEY: You took from the club and you took from the fans…

CRAIG: I always say to me players…get in the papers for the football, not for the gossip… I am having a bit of a rough time…so if you wouldn't mind…

JOEY: I read a lot of books…inside.

CRAIG: Fantastic!

JOEY: You understand how you have been mugged off.

CRAIG: Here you should read the Cloughie book, I have heard it's/

CASEY: In football right, you have to talk to people, you have to all want the same thing and you have to develop a trust.

CRAIG: Most important thing and if you haven't got trust…

JOEY: Then you're fucked!

(Beat.)

CASEY: Clubs came about because it was a decent working-class…

JOEY: A geezer's thing to do, a way to escape the pain of being…alienated labour.

CRAIG: Not just about…

JOEY: Dosh!

CRAIG: Professional footballers always paid more than the fans Joey…

JOEY: You think all the fans are scum and not the twelfth man!

CRAIG: Twelfth man definitely…without a shadow of a doubt…

JOEY: Then why does everyone steal from the twelfth man?

CASEY: *(Prompting JOEY.)* Why do you not play my brother/

BILLY: BILLY WILLIAMS BWAI!

CRAIG: *(Out of the healing reality.)* I want to stop now!

JOEY: Sometimes I felt that I had nothing to…

CASEY: Go on mate…

JOEY: Live for except my team… I didn't get into God or other geezers in the nick, like some willy flickers do… I had nothing to exist for at times…except my club… watching them on the box…

Going to me first match when I was seven, taking myself there…all on me own. Talking to strangers, all of us different, but all of us united. Stopped me being so shy and I could let me emotions out…

ALL: WHO ARE YOU? WHO ARE YOU?

JOEY: THE FUCKING GROUND IS THE ONLY PLACE I FEEL FUCKING ACCEPTED IN MY OWN COUNTRY – DO YOU GET THAT? DO YOU GET THAT CRAIG?

CASEY: What do you remember about the Eighties Joey?

JOEY: Maggie promised us everything…

CASEY: The humiliation of being born poor…of not being wanted?

JOEY: And if you are at the bottom of the pile, it's your own bleedin' fault…

ALL: SIGN ON, SIGN ON, WITH A PEN IN YOUR HAND!

CRAIG: We are done…

(JOEY turning and right in CRAIG's face.)

JOEY: We can fuck it all up, and everyone will kick off some more, run riot some fucking more…fucking let's have some, everyone's doing it…stealing/

ALL: COME AN' AVE A GO IF YOU THINK YER HARD ENOUGH, YOU'RE GOING HOME IN A FUCKING AMBULANCE!

CASEY: Billy should be starting every game mate, the fans know, in their hearts, what's right…

(JOEY touches CRAIG.)

JOEY: There's more where this…

(CRAIG releases his arm.)

CRAIG: That was…no touching; I said no touching… I SAID NO TOUCHING ME!

JOEY: We have been shat on enough…everyone shits on us… we ave nothing to lose…

(CRAIG gets JOEY by the throat.)

CRAIG: I want you all to leave…

CASEY: Do you feel released, do you feel whole…

JOEY:

(CRAIG lets go of JOEY, CRAIG walks out of the room.)

JOEY: *(Shocked, then the revelation comes.)* Casey I could do what you do!

CASEY: Billy won't have to leave the club and he will be alright, if you let me deal with it mate…

BILLY: *(Watching CRAIG go.)* For real…

CASEY: Yeah!

(To us. CASEY on her phone, striding into the club, FRANK is in his office. TONY and his team very strong.)

CASEY: Back at the ground to get a meeting with Frank –

TONY: Forty-eight points!

FRANK: Argue her Whitechapel case from a different perspective; try to retrieve our old working relationship?

TONY: Frank's busy, fifty-one /

CASEY: Points and Premiership Players here on loan!

(CASEY blocked.)

JOEY: And Casey wearing tighter clothing...fifty-four!

TONY: Trying anything – fifty-seven!

BILLY: Because, well, ears in the dressing room, and me tagged bro...

TONY: Sixty/

CASEY: I had to find a way through the mounting...insanity...

TONY: *(To the fans.)* Winning streak...

CASEY: A way through to the end of all of this...

TONY: Sixty-three...

FRANK: Back to the money...back to try and see...

TONY: Sixty-six and still third!

CASEY: Frank!

TONY: *(Looking at FATIMA.)* Sixty-nine?

FATIMA: *(Giving in.)* Seventy-one points.

CASEY: Back to see...and finally...

TONY: Seventy-four points and...we drop to fifth...but we are...

ALL: GOING UP, GOING UP, GOING UP!

(The scene. FRANK watching football, LIANNE enters, CASEY watches from a distance.)

FRANK: Lianne just landed on my desk…

LIANNE: Hello!

FRANK: A present from someone!

ALL: GOING DOWN, GOING DOWN, GOING DOWN!

(LIANNE goes towards him.)

LIANNE: Does being viewed as legit, one of us now, feel hard and sexy Mr Wong?

FRANK: *(Stroking LIANNE's hair.)* Before some quality cod, my cockerney fish cake…

LIANNE: How much money did you really make Frank, for soft loaning this club…talk football funds and business to me…offshore projects and everything… I want to learn, need to learn… Please teach me Frankie, you can hurt me baby and be my teacher!

(LIANNE giggles, and gets out her drugs.)

FRANK: The chav, who aged seven, had notions of being a beautiful princess, will swallow slowly and…

(LIANNE stumbles into CASEY. The scene, football footage fades.)

CASEY: The memories/nightmares start to come…

LIANNE: My mate made a million from one night in a hotel – bought her mum a house with the money the players paid her off with…

CASEY: How much did the tabloids offer her?

LIANNE: I have been with two hundred and fifty-six players, four managers, twelve assistant managers, three agents, a groundsman, but he smelt, a player's dad and grandad, and three in administration. And you know what?

CASEY: What…

LIANNE: I've never had an injunction.

CASEY: No minimum wage for you/

LIANNE: Unlike my sisters, because my stock is well rising and I have well learnt my craft!

CASEY: Your website is out there!

(Beat.)

All your girls branded with the St George tattoos…

LIANNE: Well I am rethinking that idea…what with the team being so consistently shite and of course the shifting demographic of our market.

CASEY: Perfect and teeth whitened…

LIANNE: All in a young packaged size ten, that's Lianne's Lovelies!

CASEY: How's your child?

LIANNE: *(Shocked.)* What's it to you?

CASEY: Safe yeah?

LIANNE: Don't look down at me ok…start to have some respect for me alright, know your boundaries…and start to have some fucking respect...

CASEY: I do!

LIANNE: We will do anything and if Frankie likes it really really rough *(Shouting.)* Shanika!

(SHANIKA/BILLY walks into the scene, he/she is also completely naked, SHANIKA and LIANNE start to perform for CASEY.)

SHANIKA: Alright?

CASEY: I want you both to leave now.

SHANIKA: Wong loves his bit of black and white!

(They both start to laugh.)

CASEY: Look, just protect yourselves alright…

LIANNE: I've got a mum!

SHANIKA: Yeah…

LIANNE: Our mummies do the little bits of admin for us…
Mummy is part of our team!

CASEY: Get out please!

SHANIKA: Frigid…

LIANNE: Scared!

(LIANNE and SHANIKA exit, CASEY doesn't think this is the right time to speak to FRANK. She turns to us, receiving a text message, back on the phone and making her way over to BILLY's crib.)

CASEY: MY EARS NO WHERE NEAR THE DRESSING
ROOM was completely doing things that would/

FRANK: Seriously come back on you Casey…

TOMMY: Seventy-five/

TONY: Tony was on the money in terms of BILLY BOY…

CASEY: For the Barking Knight had post the *healing* session…

(BILLY steps forward.)

BILLY: Deep in shame man.

CASEY: Joey obviously was nowhere to be seen, and I had to
quickly pick up the pieces…placate and…

BILLY: MAKE ME BETTER!

FRANK: Sedate him?

(The scene. CASEY closes her phone and tiptoes into BILLY's room. BILLY hides in a corner.)

BILLY: Sometimes the last thing I want to do is be a footballer,
go out onto the pitch, fans calling me a half-caste cunt, with
their mouths full of…

CASEY: Overpriced pies, I know darling, I…

   Come on bedtime Billy babe!

BILLY: Card schools, the horses, greyhounds…it got to me. EVERYTHING GOT TO ME. And did anyone try to save Billy Boy…was anyone there for me…

CASEY: Shush now…take the shoes off and put some pyjamas on!

(He gets ready for bed.)

BILLY: Don't care I only have six houses, all of them in Romford.

We are free, we control the dressing room and me control the game Gaffer.

(She wipes his tears; he then wants to sit on CASEY's lap, like a little boy, like the child, the baby she never ever had. Slowly she starts to sing.)

CASEY: Maybe it's because I'm a…

BILLY: Londoner…that I love/

CASEY: London Town…

(CASEY gives him a nod, as if to say time for bed, he obeys.)

BILLY: Why have I got so much money?

CASEY: Demand curve for strikers is inelastic…

BILLY:

CASEY: It's what the current market values and there are not many people who can put the ball in the back of the net…

(CASEY strokes his hair, he wants to be told a story, he gets out his well-travelled storybook, gives it to CASEY. We are aware of the moon/the satellites high up in the night sky, tender.)

CASEY: Jean Marc Bosman was just an ordinary Belgian Boy, but he had a dream, a dream to play football in France!

Now things weren't going exactly to plan and he was a very miserable Belgian Boy, because

BILLY: His club didn't want him to go did they…?

CASEY: So FC Liege: Belgian Boy's angry home club used this nasty horrible rule and put an enormous price tag on him, asking for money that Dunkirk, the club that Belgian Boy dreamed of playing for, obviously didn't have. So Bosman finds his/

BILLY: Balls/

CASEY: Finds his big big strength and takes them all to the big big court.

BILLY: All?

CASEY: The club, the powers-that-be in Belgium and the European football people. Belgian Boy's case being that ordinary, good EU boys were not being allowed to play, where they wanted to play…

BILLY: I like the bit where he wins…

CASEY: The world was now Belgian Boy's oyster Billy Boy, the players were now very strong and powerful, and there was no going back. Anywhere a player dreamed of playing, they could play and no transfer fee was payable, when their contract had finished…

BILLY: Could you read me the Justin story…

CASEY: The players could now be right in there now doing their own deals, and when their contracts were coming to an end, if they were still brilliant, still being picked (and not being insane), they could call all the shots, and all their childhood dreams could come true…

BILLY: Like me…

(CASEY kisses his head. She puts down the book; he snuggles up to her, close to her breast, like a fragile babe. He starts to slowly unbutton her blouse.)

CASEY: Not everyone loves Bosman though, y'know that Billy don't yer?

BILLY: Players and agents have it all now innit...

(He makes his way into her bra.)

CASEY: Exactly...

BILLY: You've got it all, haven't you mummy?

(She stops him from sucking her nipple, FRANK suddenly behind her.)

FRANK: Seventy-six points.

CASEY: Sorry, but I've got to go, I've got to catch a plane mate!

(CASEY quickly back in Africa, at the bottom of BILLY's bed... Talking to a slightly drunk TOMMY and waiting for MOUFTY, whilst again on her phone.)

CASEY: More players, ok more contradictions on my part, more pissing off Michel...but/

TOMMY: *(Holding back the tears.)* Tony Whitechapel banged my missus too...

(Big beat.)

CASEY: And more signings to keep Frank's interest...

TOMMY: *(Chanting in FRANK's voice.)* Who are you, who are you, who are you?

(MOUFTY enters, CASEY closes her phone.)

TOMMY: Didn't tell us Razak pisses his bed did yer grandad?

MOUFT: What did you think of the boys?

TOMMY: She didn't wanna buy anything.

MOUFT: Pascal is a genius/

TOMMY: Don't tell me you had Arsene out here himself last week?

MOUFT: Take Nouham and Pascal for free…

CASEY: Look I might take Romuald.

TOMMY: Same set up as your Razak…

MOUFT: I do have another match organized…if you could just stay…slightly longer…

(CASEY gets up, back on the phone.)

TOMMY: Razak is being sent back, you will have to pay for his flight!

CASEY: Razak was one of seven boys I took a gamble on…not everyone…not every kid makes it…

MOUFT: You will take Romuald; he is good, really very good.

(CASEY looks around, unable to see MOUFTAOU's new wife.)

TOMMY: *(Aside.)* You will be offering us your fucking goats next nigger!

(MOUFTY goes for TOMMY, a fight, CASEY in between them. CASEY's phone bleeps, she reads a text, closes her phone. To us.)

CASEY: Result!

(CASEY collecting and putting the manuscript under her arm, running into FRANK's office. The scene.)

CASEY: Flats and cars and gifts for his various women/

FRANK: His pussy…

CASEY: All his shares are financed by illegal loans…

FRANK: Getting rich out of the transfer of injured players, like what's his name y'know…the gay Serbian we had here three years ago?

CASEY:

FRANK: If you can't remember names/

CASEY: Stories that are all in another book that is to be finally published... That is to have two chapters devoted to Anthony Whitechapel.

(She places the book in front of FRANK.)

CASEY: Tax dodges for foreigners...

FRANK: Eighty points and we are in the play offs. The Premiership is real.

CASEY: This club always paid over the odds for everyone and then sold them as...

FRANK: Something that was losing its market value?

CASEY: I have been speaking to a...

FRANK: Someone in The Met? A friendly copper?

CASEY: And he could go down for the tax evasion, very, very...but eh, you knew all this already?

FRANK: Sort out Billy Williams!

CASEY: Why didn't we have any paperwork...any proper paperwork/

FRANK: From Frank? From me, Casey...

(Silence. He goes through his information.)

FRANK: You were once a *professional* stripper!

CASEY: Tony...

FRANK: You would never be allowed to have a bush like that...in this day and age!

(To us.)

TONY: Fatima was also simultaneously trying not to entertain thoughts of killing herself, as she caught me with Lianne, Shanika and this pretty Su Li one, in the changing rooms after...

(The scene. FRANK's office cont.)

CASEY: I am trying to do something good!

FRANK: Interesting, very interesting…

CASEY: They hadn't slept for days right…

FRANK: Nobody slept where they were?

CASEY: The enemy allowed them to practice; they pushed them to practice…

FRANK: They wanted a quality game…a forty thousand gate?

CASEY: So it had to be skilled and entertaining…

FRANK: The enemy knew they had that hidden something…

CASEY: So they fed them well…

FRANK: The Landmark Hotel!

CASEY:

FRANK: The enemy also gave them clothes and they got to wear a kit that was…

CASEY: The Alexander McQueen dress you sent me…

FRANK: Cause they were holding hands in the dressing room…running out to the roar and release of the crowd

CASEY: At half-time they were winning…they were far the better team…

FRANK: Playing their hearts out, every tackle/

CASEY: Every moment mattered…

FRANK: The Ukraine against the Nazis/

CASEY: But they were being told they had to lose/

FRANK: They couldn't win and if they won then their lives…

CASEY: Their lives were at risk Frank?

FRANK: Having won the match…

CASEY: Their supporters full of hope!

FRANK: The players were transported away; the entire professional squad were then executed. I know everything sexy!

(FATIMA enters.)

FATIMA: The Italian manager wants to meet us Frank and I think we should go after Michel Gbagbo!

(To us. The team still playing.)

CASEY: Fatima wanted to talk to me now…

TONY: Casey agreed to meet me after the match…

FRANK: Made a few calls…

TONY: Semi-finals play off – first leg!

CASEY: I was shaking…inside.

MICHEL: She wasn't listening!

JOEY: I told Billy I wanted to represent him…proper like!

BILLY: She had let me down again!

CASEY: I have never once underestimated the resilience of darkness…

MICHEL: The resilience…

FRANK: Of all this...

ALL: A draw!

(The scene: CASEY and a suited and booted very handsome TONY, barely any light.)

TONY: Today I am sitting in a café right, all alone and… drinking me tea…and I gets a call…a call from the consortium and they want to offer me a job…

CASEY: A man is a man for what he contributes to football… what he contributes to the ninety minutes…

TONY: They talked various positions… Leeds, Cardiff, Crystal Palace…

CASEY:

TONY: But I have a job, I have a club…

CASEY: Bet the money's nice…

TONY: Money is very nice indeed and there would be…

CASEY: Extras…

TONY: I don't know what to say…take your pick they say… keep in football…

CASEY: Keep in the game…

TONY: They told me to talk about it with you…

CASEY: The agent girl…

TONY: They told me to tell you to…

CASEY: What?

TONY: Do you…

CASEY: What?

TONY: I remember that night around 1983…

CASEY: When you told me there was no join…

TONY: You remember that night…don't you Casey…tell me you still remember? When you let me…stay in you all night?

CASEY: You said you loved me.

TONY: You loved the attention from all the lads, and you were…up for anything…tell us you were?

CASEY: Damaged, before I was delivered to you?

TONY: I cried stay away, stay away from me please... Stay away from the game! Stay away from the game now!

CASEY: Are *you* threatening me?

TONY: NO!

(To us, CASEY moves away and phones MICHEL, team play football.)

MICHEL: Judge not your beauty by the number of people who look at you, but rather by the number of people who smile at you/

CASEY: You need to get a move on babe, I'm…

MICHEL: Was or never will be your country's black Beckham. I am not English and I am African… Frank doesn't want me…

CASEY: Second leg…

JOEY: A better Billy Williams back on the side.

MICHEL: Everywhere is a sea of white!

CASEY: Am so close darling…everything is nearly falling into place…magic is happening!

MICHEL: I don't believe you…

CASEY: The planets are aligning sweetheart!

MICHEL: You are a liar…

CASEY: Tell me what I have done!

MICHEL: Have friends in *your* team!

CASEY: That's great.

MICHEL: There's this kid, wandering around outside *your* ground, goes by the name of Razak, has nothing but his clothes in a blue carrier bag, says you promised him the world, has no flight home, no money! The skinny boy is stranded…

CASEY: We have to go back to go forward…We have to go back to be honest with ourselves…conscious…powerful and free!

MICHEL: You are not making any sense…

CASEY: Zola was thirty-nine. Just get on a plane now please; we can make things work when you get here *(Receiving a text.)* we are in the final!

TONY: *(Looking at FRANK.)* Nice one!

MICHEL: Sort out the Razak situation!

(He hangs up. CASEY at her favourite restaurant. The team act as waiters, to us.)

CASEY: Fatima had been invited out for dinner!

FATIMA: Layton still on her mission/

FRANK: Was still holding it all together…

TONY: Impressive…but both stupid, very/

(FATIMA enters. The scene.)

CASEY: We had got together at a do that I was taken to by my dad…

FATIMA:

CASEY: Anthony had just been signed and asked me out/

FATIMA:

CASEY: He held parties at his flat and people drank Martini.

FATIMA:

CASEY: Anthony had three of his mates round, one evening… all of them on the edge of the first team, and having lost in the reserves that day…

WAITER/JOEY: Would madam like some wine?

FATIMA:

CASEY: The Boys very drunk decided to play cards and again I wasn't allowed to join in, I fell asleep on the sofa…

FATIMA:

CASEY: Anthony, having lost all night, and off his face…
agreed that he would gamble me next…

FATIMA:

WAITER/BILLY: Can I get you both anything?

CASEY: I am on Anthony's mum's plastic but leather looking
sofa, and I am being woken up, and I am having all my
clothes taken off me… I am struggling to break free…
screaming for Anthony's mates to stop, then the soon to be
goalie's groin pressing into me…and then I am naked and
Anthony is standing in the corner and Anthony's eyes are
dead and he can't really stand, and he is just staring and
the left back calls him over to help to hold me down…and
he shouts come on Anthony…come on, cause they wanted
him to represent…

FATIMA: I think I should be going…

WAITER/TONY: Do you want me to call you/

CASEY: I just look across and out of the window…out of the
net curtains onto his street and because the mind always
seeks to equilibrate in a moment of crisis…I imagine other
things…nice things like my Nan who I knew really loved
me and then they all including Anthony fuck me…

FATIMA: What do you want me to say?

CASEY: I was an expansion of the goal, that they didn't score
that day. A late celebration they needed to have, and
Anthony/

WAITER/TONY: Do you want me to call you a cab?

CASEY: I went home…pregnant, but lost the child pretty early
on. *(Beat.)* I moved across London and got a job in a…

FATIMA: The sex industry.

CASEY: And some will say it all served me?

FATIMA: What if you went to court?

CASEY: Where would I be…who would I be…without this great story…

FATIMA: Rape serves?

CASEY: A divine order!

FATIMA: Don't fuck up your life like Casey Layton – don't waste all those years hating?

CASEY: Frightened…silent!

FATIMA: I know where Tony keeps his paperwork.

CASEY: What do you know about Frank Wong?

FATIMA: The consortium?

WAITER/FRANK: Anything wrong ladies?

(To us, phone activity.)

MICHEL: Casey texted me.

CASEY: Three goals!

MICHEL: *(Reading her text.)* Sorry and want to love you… But I am still vulnerable and very messed up/

CASEY: And yes scared/

MICHEL: *(Still reading.)* Help me Michel please…

CASEY: PROTECT ME!

MICHEL: GBAGBO WAS GETTING ON A PLANE.

CASEY: Linda died in the night.

(The scene.)

BILLY: We won the play-off finals.

JOEY: Got a hat-trick bro!

BILLY: Get on the phone to Barcelona!

MICHEL: The club was promoted.

CASEY: Madness…

MICHEL: It's all going to be alright.

(LIANNE, JOEY & FRANK pile onto BILLY to celebrate his hat-trick.)

ALL: GOING UP, GOING UP, GOING UP!

(Some football plays, old tapes of TONY, which he comes and watches on his grand telly. A bottle of whiskey is beside WHITECHAPEL, he his now drinking heavily. FATIMA enters, she searches cupboards, under the bed, all is turned frantically upside down.

CASEY is given a dossier, this documents key Premiership moments. This is followed by FRANK and his family's global activities and then the subsequent slaughter of many villagers, under the guise of the war on drugs, in Northern Thailand. What CASEY is studiously reading about, we see images of, on the football screens. Her fear is palpable. The following domestic plays over the images.)

FATIMA: And I still kept the key to our flat…

TONY: She's dead… Linda died…

FATIMA: Exhausted/

TONY: This hurts…

FATIMA: Unloved.

TONY: Just stay with me for a bit…please?

FATIMA: YOU HAVE TO DO SOMETHING ON YOUR OWN FOR ONCE…

TONY: Could you get me a little glass of water…

FATIMA: Where's your brown box? Where's your brown box arsehole? Where's the new stuff from the Consortium? *(FATIMA goes to him pulling back his hair.)* White trash! You are nothing but white fucking trash, remember that Tony, every day when you look in the mirror, remember that Anthony Whitechapel!

(FATIMA lets his head go and continues to search, images continue to play, time passes.)

TONY: She was pretty, older than me, but pretty.

FATIMA: She was bald and she was smoking sixty a day.

TONY: SAID SORRY AND I SAID I WAS STAYING, I SAID I CAN'T SAY ANYMORE SORRYS LINDA, I CAN'T SAY ANYMORE SORRYS…THIS IS ALL INSANE!

FATIMA: *(Speaking as LINDA.)* Who am I Anthony…who am I now? What did all the frocks mean then? What is a woman to you? Explain wife to me… Footballer's wife? WAG… You can't tell the difference can yer?

TONY: Linda!

FATIMA: AND IT IS TONY, WHO IS NOT ONLY KILLING THE GAME, BUT KILLING TONY…

TONY: Not the biggest killer…

(Silence. FATIMA now has everything, CASEY is now very much the main focus.)

TONY: Get me some water please…

FATIMA: *(Looking at the box.)* Everything you hid… *(Looking around the room.)* the dreams we had, I feel so unclean, so hugely soiled.

TONY: You were only ever out for yourself…

FATIMA: I know what you did to Casey, when you were seventeen…

TONY: How did you get involved in all this?

FATIMA: Got to go see her…

TONY: Fatima!

(CASEY stops reading, FATIMA leaves and is met by some of FRANK's men. A plane lands. The scene. CASEY and MICHEL on the move.)

MICHEL: Straight to Frank?

CASEY: Seeing you in the flesh, will make him change his mind, it will be good for the press!

MICHEL: *(Stopping walking.)* I have missed you!

(He goes to put his arm around her.)

CASEY: Not here!

(LIANNE enters.)

LIANNE: Getting some stuff for The Gaffer…

CASEY: Leave as quickly as you can please…

LIANNE: Sad about his wife, but/

CASEY: Sport goes on…

(LIANNE proceeds to rub herself up against MICHEL.)

CASEY: Lianne!

LIANNE: Baby, I want you!

MICHEL: This isn't a good time…

LIANNE: *(Rubbing her nose.)* Fill me up!

MICHEL: This isn't a turn-on…

LIANNE: My card gorgeous…

MICHEL: *(Breaking free.)* Don't think err…

LIANNE: I never fail to bring any man on this planet, to his knees…

(To MICHEL.) Don't make me and all my girls wait too long…

(MICHEL looks at the card, CASEY looks at MICHEL, he doesn't take the business card. All the players take up their positions and FRANK speaks to Sky Sports, CASEY beside FRANK, again all very proper. Woman in wheelchair nearby, somewhat neglected.)

FRANK: Look, I am not into burning candles on the pitch, multi-faith and multi-cultural love-ins…but I do want us all to say a prayer for Anthony Whitechapel at this sad time and/

(Cut.)

It is fantastic to be able to interest the likes of Gbagbo to this club. I have always admired his great striking talent, speed on the ball, and of course remarkable intelligence/ For as we start in The Premiership, we have to be realistic, and understand it will be hard. At times we will have to sacrifice the beauty of our football for simply getting results…

(Cut.)

Hurst talks about the first domestic home game after the world cup and those three boys coming back to their manor/

(Cut.)

I will look at the season ticket price issue, and more fans forums will be part of the calendar.

(Cut.)

If I could share with you all just an old proverb, something from my native culture… *(Proceeding to speak in standard Mandarin.)*

A good fortune may forbade a bad luck, which may in turn disguise a good fortune.

*(The scene, music starts to play. All major players mingle; FRANK takes to the dancefloor and starts to do his rendition of **Can't Take My Eyes Off You**. He sings well and FRANK's employees applaud enthusiastically; everyone is having a blinding time. CASEY goes towards BILLY, JOEY and LIANNE, FRANK speaking, possibly playing on a loop. JOEY and BILLY come forward to meet her. LIANNE is hanging off BILLY.)*

JOEY: Got me indemnity insurance…

BILLY: Comes into the toilet with me…

CASEY: Like all good agents should!

LIANNE: Billy asked me to marry him!

BILLY: She said yes!

JOEY: Brings tears to my eyes…

(LIANNE and BILLY kiss. CASEY moves towards FRANK.)

FRANK: Fatima delivered, directly to me…

CASEY: False accounting, fraud, everything Tony got up to?

(Beat.)

Where is she?

FRANK: You don't want to know where Fatima is and nobody wants a media frenzy… Gbagbo is obese…

(CASEY walks over to MICHEL.)

MICHEL: You can't even look me in the eye…

CASEY: Nobody is looking anyone in the eye Michel…

MICHEL: Eyes…all in the eyes…for/

(TONY enters.)

TONY: *(He stands on a chair.)* I know, you all think I am the biggest villain, but you got it all wrong, all very wrong… but ok make Tony the whipping boy…

MICHEL: So you finally got all that you wanted?

CASEY: *(She looks MICHEL in the eye.)* I am bad news…sorry!

MICHEL: Razak?

CASEY: Michel!

MICHEL: Frank doesn't want me here. You're not interested. *(Beat.)* Why did I ever think anything could be any different? I am going back to Spain.

CASEY: I will explain.

(MICHEL leaves.)

TONY: Come on everyone…come on…whipping boy here!

And who hasn't been shouted at, spat at…

Last of the fucking English…

(He takes off his belt. He offers it to the crowd, offers it to CASEY. FRANK slowly makes his way over to TONY.)

FRANK: Tony can I have a word…

TONY: *(Falling off the chair.)* Just make me the…

FRANK: Eh you got us into The Premiership!

CASEY: Well done Anthony…

ALL: Gaffer!

FRANK: You can stay!

(FRANK and the crowd applaud TONY. FRANK moves towards CASEY, they both move away from the crowd. They are suddenly in a bedroom.)

FRANK: *(Taking off his tie, sitting on the bed.)* Told you we would have the most expensive room tonight!

CASEY: You're a married man Frank.

FRANK: She's on the other side of the world.

CASEY: In prison.

FRANK: So? *(He wants her to sit on the bed.)*

CASEY: You have a lot of passports.

FRANK: I was born in Burma, its politics, it's complicated.

CASEY: Trafficking in so many things.

FRANK: When are you going to finally embrace what you are?

(She starts to massage him.)

CASEY: Alright Adolf.

FRANK: Don't be the second person this evening, to make a complete fool of themselves.

CASEY:

FRANK: The internet is…

CASEY: Not to be trusted…

FRANK: Exactly…

CASEY: Your satellite company, illegal stock trading and the global tax evasion…

FRANK: I have a Cayman Island bank account, who doesn't!

CASEY: Contravening every single human right…

FRANK: Survival…

CASEY: Lots of people are investigating…

(FRANK riled.)

FRANK: You keep forgetting you were my choice, and you were too consumed with righting the past, that you forgot to keep up with the present. A common flaw. Like everyone in football, like everyone who watches, we only see what we want to see.

CASEY: So I got what I deserved?

FRANK: If anyone in this game was truly a *Wenger* third way type of human being, they wouldn't really be working in all of this at all.

CASEY: You employ the best legal team and accountants possible, to make sure it works for you.

FRANK: And everyone has lots and lots of fun. *(Beat.)* Time for some Sinatra I think!

(Music starts to play. FRANK takes CASEY by the hand, and they start to waltz.)

CASEY: Brady always says never look back…

FRANK: Brady's a clever woman!

(Looking at FRANK's money which now covers the entire stage.)

CASEY: Just to wash your money and now that your money is clean!

FRANK: Your team will just about get as many points as Derby did, eventually all will be glory fans, but whilst there is one hundred million to be made from our first and probably only year…

CASEY: You will stay.

(CASEY continues to dance with FRANK.)

FRANK: People don't want to understand that you have to have bad to have good, pain to have joy, losing to know what winning is. They don't want to experience the absoluteness of being a supporter, of being alive. And even in a time of austerity and anger/

CASEY: We have to thank modern top-flight football for maintaining illusion.

FRANK: From Gerard smiling at you when you draw your cash out of the hole in the wall, to the Chelsea weaning kits, to our amazing and sophisticated plans for the future…

It's all connected, making us all feel warm inside and connected!

Even hooker Lianne knows that football feeds on the universal lack of imagination, and the increasing desperation to globally belong and have something to get on your knees for. And until something is able to match, what football gives us all, which is of course highly unlikely, I will continue to win.

CASEY:

FRANK: And no matter how bad it gets, how rotten the game, people will always love it, always need it. Haven't I played brilliantly?

CASEY: Yes.

FRANK: I won! I won! I won!

CASEY: People will continue to investigate; it will catch up with you.

FRANK: You could have made some serious money, but you asked too many questions.

CASEY: Some things are worth more than money Frank.

(FRANK now very eager for CASEY.)

FRANK: Come on…

CASEY:

FRANK: You always knew who you were getting in bed with…

CASEY:

FRANK: I want my trophy, then fish and chips!

(CASEY gets up, she leaves. Time passes, extra time, to us. A press conference.)

CASEY: If I had a tip eleven/

FRANK: A new consortium running the club, could be better for everyone.

JOEY: Frank can't stay forever…

TONY: There's no money for players…my hands are tied.

FRANK: Francesco, the Italian will look after you all…

TONY: I am very excited about the managerial challenge of… Cambodia.

FRANK: I am sorry, but my countries need me.

JOEY: Relegation battle…

BILLY: Surrey is the place to live bwai!

JOEY: Twelve bedrooms!

FIT AND PROPER PEOPLE

LIANNE: Lickkle baby on the way and a magazine deal!

(Beat.)

It was my childhood dream to be an interior designer.

BILLY/LIANNE: LOVE!

BILLY: Telling my bredren on the streets, to grow up and behave themselves man!

MICHEL: Our centre should be open in about six months

(Beat.)

I think long distance relationships can work.

JOEY: Holding up the table...

TONY: Fatima...who?

ALL: Sorry to hear that/ please send my condolences/ such a waste...

FRANK: English batter, I will miss the English batter!

JOEY: *(To the fans.)* This club will be alright...

(CASEY turning and looking at FRANK, grabbing his microphone.)

CASEY: Because some things are worth dying for!

(Blackout. Gunshot.)